A Voice for Those
Bereaved by Suicide

A Voice for Those
Bereaved by Suicide

Sarah McCarthy

VERITAS

Published 2001 by
Veritas Publications
7/8 Lower Abbey Street
Dublin 1
Ireland

Email publications@veritas.ie
Website www.veritas.ie

ISBN 1 85390 593 3

A catalogue record for this book is available from the British Library.

Veritas books are printed on paper made from the wood pulp of managed forests. For every tree felled, at least one tree is planted, thereby renewing natural resources.

Cover design by Pierce Design
Printed in the Republic of Ireland by Leinster Leader.

Dedicated to my children

CONTENTS

INTRODUCTION

ALL TOO OFTEN in our society, those bereaved by suicide are denied the opportunity to speak freely and openly about how the death of a loved one has affected them. This is very unfortunate, as those grieving can benefit enormously if they can only share their pain and have their numerous and various fears alleviated. In writing of my own experience of a husband's suicide, I have tried to become a voice for all those who haven't been heard, and to foster a greater awareness of all who have been in some way touched by such a tragic loss.

CHAPTER ONE

A Husband's Suicide

HEARING THE NEWS of my husband's suicide was a shattering experience. It was news that I had been both dreading and preparing myself to receive for some time. When it came, however, I discovered that it had been impossible to prepare myself for that moment; it turned my life upside down and changed it forever.

On hearing the news I could feel fear rising inside of me. I replaced the receiver and a wave of blind panic swept over me. My heart started to pound, my mouth became dry and my breath left me. I felt dizzy and wanted to be sick. As the seconds ticked by terrible images began to flash through my mind. Feelings of helplessness and hopelessness overwhelmed me and I longed to be able to turn the clock back and have a different outcome. I scanned the faces of my four small children and tried desperately to find the sensible and necessary words for telling them that their daddy was dead.

From that point on my memories are a little hazy, but I know that the children watched my expressions closely and took their cues from me. If they saw that I could be sad, cry and be upset, but still able to cope and be in control, then they would be able to do so as well. I can only guess at their pain and confusion. In order to comfort them I told them to think of their father as being safe and warm with God. At every available opportunity I hugged the children and tried to get them on my own. This proved rather difficult, as soon the household became filled with extended family members, friends, work colleagues, neighbours and clergy. The entire house was soon buzzing with people discussing my husband's suicide, yet nobody could give me an answer to why it had to happen.

When my husband died he was only in his thirties and the children's ages ranged from ten to two years. To the outside world it seemed as if he had everything to live for. He had his physical health, he had a wife and four beautiful children, two boys and two girls. He was at the top of his profession and commanded a salary that ensured a very comfortable lifestyle. Yet all of this was not enough for my husband's well-being.

Being a high achiever, my late husband always strove for perfection and became frustrated, angry, impatient and intolerant when any signs of imperfection were detectable in anything or in anyone, especially in himself. It was as if he were spiritually dead. He was a man who could not contemplate the possibility of failure and he continually set himself tasks and goals in order to test and prove his abilities.

When I met my husband we were both students. He was nearly four years older than I and was everything I wished for in a partner. He was intelligent, well-mannered, gentle, kind and goal orientated. Our courtship years were happy and carefree. We had a great bunch of friends who were like-minded and we were as one big extended family. There was never a cross word spoken between us and when I qualified as a nurse we were married.

The wedding was a happy affair and I joked with my father that he was rushing me down the aisle instead of walking at the normal leisurely pace. Had I known then what was in front of me I would have turned around and had my father rush me out of the church – to freedom!

Soon after our wedding another side of my husband emerged. It was a controlling, aggressive side, which chilled me to the bone. He didn't want me to go out without him, he didn't want my friends in the house, he was downright rude to people who just popped in or who phoned wanting to speak with me. In my naivety I thought that once the children came along he would change and become more relaxed and less defensive. If anything, when the children did come, he seemed to become even more controlling, demanding to know how I'd spent my days and moaning non-stop about my lack of housewife and cooking skills. Nothing I did was right and every day it seemed as if I walked on eggshells in case I'd upset him.

He even checked the mileage on the car. If his mood was bad enough he'd tell me to turn off the television or to get out of a seat as his money had paid for everything. He'd sneer when I read a newspaper or a book saying that I hadn't the intelligence to understand what was written in them. Repeatedly I was told that I was nothing without him and that I'd only married him for a free meal-ticket for life.

What wasn't permissible for me, however, did not apply to him. I was never allowed to question him or to ask even simple everyday inquiries without being accused of having Gestapo-like tendencies. The very odd time when he wasn't behaving like a tyrant he could be 'Mr Charm' himself. He spoke with pride about the children, even stating that they were such great children that we should have some more. He spoke of their blue-eyed, blond beauty and of their intelligence and lovable natures.

During these changing times I would still sometimes see the man of our courtship days, and I'd be lulled into a false sense of security. I kept up appearances for family and friends, hoping that all would be well, and convinced myself that the situation wasn't as bad as I'd imagined. It soon became apparent that after such pleasant episodes the nastier side of his personality would emerge even stronger and more intense. All the goodness would be wiped away by vicious outbursts and vile words. I cringe when I recall some of the names and actions that he attributed to me.

I mentally began to distance myself from my husband and switched off from him. I decided that there wasn't much left that my husband could do to cause even more pain and hurt, so I decided that I could rise above him. I functioned as well as I could, but leaving him didn't seem a possibility for several reasons. I had no money of my own, and held strongly the belief that marriage was for life. I was young and inexperienced in worldly matters, with four small children dependent upon me. My extended family would not have been in favour of a separation. But the main reason why I didn't leave my husband then was that I was confused, totally isolated, and blaming myself for my husband's behaviour. I definitely was suffering from learned helplessness, a condition where the victim doesn't see that there's a way out of a bad situation and they feel stuck and decisionless.

I busied myself with the children, the home and the tending of a large garden. Close friends visited or phoned when my husband was either working or playing golf. They never judged me or told me what to do, they just accepted the fact that my husband was a little strange, bad tempered, odd and eccentric. They knew to keep out of his way for my sake as well as for their own. It has been said that you don't lose a person in one go, but rather you lose them by degrees, and this is exactly what was happening to me. I felt that I was slowly losing myself, bit by bit.

My individuality, my self-esteem and self-respect were all dissolving and melting away, and I did not like what was being left behind. The turning point came for me when my husband's drinking became so out of hand that he'd pass out and not remember where he'd been or where he was. He was arrested for drunk driving and his outbursts frightened the children. He began to threaten suicide as, according to him, 'Life was just far too difficult'.

I overcame my reservation about not speaking openly about my husband and made an appointment to talk with a local clergyman. This appointment was the first step in reclaiming myself. This particular clergyman gave me the time and space that enabled me to stand back from the situation and gain a wider perspective on everything. He patiently sat in silence when I was too upset to do any talking. The tears flowed from me and I experienced from this wonderful person a sense of positive regard in a non-judgmental stance. It can only be described as being an unconditional spiritual love. Through my many meetings with this clergyman I became strong again and more focused. I saw paths opening up for me where before I saw only blocked walls and closed doors.

After finding my confidence and renewed awareness, I spoke with our general practitioner, close friends and work colleagues of my husband. In fact, I knocked on every door that I felt help could come from. The response was always the same. I was told that unless my husband sought help for himself then there was nothing that could be done.

I'd regularly find empty and full bottles of alcohol hidden around the house and in the car. My husband no longer wanted to eat with us or even be in the same room. Often he'd lock himself in his study and demand that his meals be left outside of the door. All reasoning and pleading fell on deaf ears, and in my heart I knew that disaster was ahead. Events were out of my control and all I could do was hope and pray that God would help and guide me. My husband's rages and outbursts became more and more alarming. He'd kick holes in doors, smash up furniture and empty turf bags around the home.

Life was very, very difficult for me knowing that my husband would not let anyone close enough to help him. My decision to separate from him was one that I didn't make lightly. I had to protect the children and myself and somehow make him aware of his actions and be accountable for them. I was aware that it would take a very special person to confront my husband and offer him the help he so desperately needed.

Finding a good solicitor was easy and everything seemed to fall into place for me. A legal separation was granted, with a monthly maintenance made payable to the courts set in motion. A mortgage was arranged and the children and myself moved to a beautiful small bungalow that provided a sense of security, comfort and safety. When I told my husband my plans to move he assured me that it was what he'd longed for – to be free of us and our demands on him. He longed to be able to 'do his own thing'. I told him that while we loved and cared for him we could no longer live with him as he was destroying all that was good around him. I encouraged him to seek help and promised that once he was better everything would be different.

After moving out of the family home I came under pressure from my own extended family and from my in-laws to 'come to my senses' and to return to my husband. I had never spoken ill of my husband to anyone and a sense of misplaced loyalty prevented me from doing so now. I just repeated over and over that my husband should be encouraged to seek professional help. Phone call after phone call came from my husband, saying 'this is goodbye for the last time', 'you'll never see or hear from me again' and 'this is all your fault'. After such calls I would become alarmed and phone close friends asking if they would call upon my husband. They would do so only to find him calmly drinking tea, denying that anything was wrong. When he was asked to give an explanation as to why I had left him he would lie, telling folk that I was having an affair.

I did not allow the children to answer the phone when it rang and I'd unplug it at night-time. This really enraged my husband and he'd often threaten to set fire to our timber framed bungalow as we slept in our beds. I was very alarmed and concerned about these threats and felt very much alone and unprotected. I kept all as normal as possible for the children, but they could not be shielded from everything, and when he demanded his rights to 'see his children', and they didn't want to be with him, he'd accuse me of poisoning their minds against him and he angrily promised that he'd punish me for it. He could not see beyond his needs and his rights and he could not see the terror in his children's eyes.

Just when I was despairing of the whole situation the unthinkable happened – my husband went to speak with the clergyman who was seeing me through this nightmare. I perceived this act as being very significant for one of two reasons: either my husband realised that he had a problem and was going to do something about it, or this visit was in the form of a last confessions – the latter was to turn out to be true.

All day prior to learning of my husband's suicide I was very unsettled, so I busied myself as best I could with the children and housework. Finally, I could bear the tension no longer and went to visit a friend expressing concerns that my husband was dead. My friend did her best to reassure me and asked her husband to check that all was well. On returning home I began to prepare the evening meal. While standing at the sink, with the water running over my hands, it suddenly felt as if a telepathic connection had been made and I felt an overwhelming sense of calm and peace flood over me. It felt as if all the struggling was over. My husband's struggle to leave this life, and mine to keep him in it. I had a sense that he had won, as in life he had tried to control me, and by his suicide he had the ultimate control over us all. I reasoned with myself that such an act of death couldn't be repeated, it was a one-off action on behalf of my husband so I didn't have to worry that he'd do it again. I comforted myself with the believe that he had found a peace in heaven that he couldn't have found on earth.

The two older children were old enough to understand the concept of death. They knew that they could never talk with or see their father again. I explained as I had done so many times previously that their daddy had loved and cared for them but that he had been very sick, and now he had taken too many tablets, which stopped his heart and breathing and caused him to die. He was now with God in heaven. I told them that none of this was their fault as God had many methods for bringing a person back to him to be healed. The eldest girl was inconsolable, but allowed herself to be comforted. The eldest boy became very quiet and said very little, but he too accepted hugs, kisses and reassurances.

The younger children became very clingy and objected strongly to not having me in sight. They had a concept of death from seeing beloved pets die and be buried, but other than that they were far too young to understand all that had occurred.

The house soon filled with extended family, friends, colleagues, clergy, neighbours and other well-wishers. The blinds were closed, the television and radio were turned off and it was as if a strange eeriness crept over the house. The silences were interrupted by the ringing of the telephone and doorbell. Chairs appeared from nowhere, and china cups, saucers and plates piled up in the kitchen. Sandwiches, biscuits and buns were handed around along with an endless supply of tea.

I felt as if I were redundant, as each time I went to stand up I was gently, but firmly, told to sit back down. I wanted to tell people that I wasn't sick; I was fine and wanted to be active. As I greeted people I felt their trembling and awkwardness as well as their shocked concern. It seemed to me that I had to comfort many well-wishers whose tears and sorrow registered on their faces. Everyone asked if they could do anything to help and I longed to say that it was too late. When close friends told me that they would be spending day and night with me until the funeral was over, I genuinely couldn't reason why – all I knew was that the danger of something happening to the children was gone and we no longer needed protection. People were being so caring and concerned now that it seemed unreal.

This sense of unreality was reinforced by the necessary police involvement, which made me feel implicated in a crime. Even though my husband's death was private and without witnesses I felt guilty by association. My in-laws further added to this sense of guilt by attributing full blame onto me for my husband's decision to take his life. To them, I had driven him to suicide. They never had accepted the fact that he was ill and in need of professional help. My in-laws made the arrangements for the funeral and burial without consulting me directly. I was only too happy to comply with their wishes, however, as it took the decision-making and burden off my shoulders, and I honestly didn't have either the energy or the desire to make my own wishes heard. In doing this my in-laws gave me the clear message that my late husband was their flesh and blood, and as I had rejected him they would bury him in their family grave.

I never like to see dead bodies, as I'd rather remember the person as he or she was when they were alive, but I was encouraged to view my husband's body and to see for myself how serene his face was in death. A very close friend came with me to the chapel of rest to say my goodbyes to my husband. He did indeed look peaceful and as if asleep, but I was very much aware that his essence wasn't present. All I could think of was that beneath the sheet that covered him his body had undergone a post-mortem, which established exactly how he had killed himself.

The funeral service and burial were also very sad and distressful experiences. I was glad to have my brother's and my close friends' support throughout. My husband's family had taken over the front rows of the church so the children and myself had to sit halfway down the church. This, to me, was a very unfeeling and a revengeful public display of their dismissal of us as being prominent mourners. I could feel the full force of their collective vindictiveness and rage. I tried to focus on what the clergyman was saying, but as he was unknown to me and had never met my late husband, his words seemed somewhat hollow. Having to stand by my husband's grave with my children and shake hands with so many people required every ounce of endurance that I possessed. All I longed for was to return home and be away from all public scrutiny. I was physically and emotionally drained, and so very cold.

Mourners and well-wishers were invited for a meal at the nearest hotel, but I couldn't face being sociable, so my brother and sister represented me while I returned home with the children, a beloved aunt, a dear cousin and a close friend. We were in the warmth and shared soup and sandwiches with sweetened tea. We opened up the window shades, which symbolically signalled the ending of the darkness and the bringing in of freshness and light.

Lying in bed that night, with the two little ones snuggled up beside me, I thought of how the situation could have turned out much worse. My children were safe and secure now, and I made a silent promise to rear them in love to the very best of my ability, and to help them overcome the tragedy in their young lives.

CHAPTER TWO

Approaching Those Bereaved by Suicide

THERE IS NOTHING more uplifting for those who are left feeling despondent, disillusioned and distraught following the suicide of a loved one than to have someone who radiates light into their darkened world. When clergy, relatives, friends and colleagues visit a household recently bereaved by suicide they bring with them not only the warmth of human kindness but also the light of hope.

I was left struggling in my attempts to make sense of my husband's seemingly meaningless and senseless act. I felt abandoned, as if I was part of an atrocity against the very sacredness of life itself. People who took the time to offer support, guidance, understanding and acceptance during these early stages of grief are recalled with a special gratitude. I remember all who came to the house, and, indeed, all who didn't come.

While it is never easy to witness pain and suffering in others, or even to know how best to approach those in grief without either saying or doing something to cause further upset, it is possible to make approaching those in grief a little easier. Helping those recently bereaved by a suicide goes beyond the following of a few simple rules. It involves a knowledge and understanding of grief, as well as warmth, empathic dedication, compassion to help others and the ability to radiate a positive, comforting reassurance of a spiritual nature. In being able to meet the special needs of those grieving their loss, would-be helpers experience the satisfaction of being truly and deeply helpful.

Bereavement by suicide requires tremendous psychological adjustment and adaptation in order for those grieving to keep relatively sound – mentally, emotionally and spiritually. The usual stages of shock, alarm, denial, anger and acceptance must be gone through, but they tend to be more prolonged and intense with many physical, psychological and spiritual symptoms. What might be considered 'normal' for one individual may not be normal for another. Raw intense emotions and feelings are all jumbled up. One minute the person is fine and the next overwhelming panic and alarm flood the body and tears flow. The pain experienced is inescapable and persuasive and leaves the bereaved struggling, depressed, anxious and even a little hostile. Mental confusion, emotional upheaval and feelings of insecurity, uncertainty and inadequacy lead to a loss of self-confidence and esteem.

Feelings of shame following a suicide leave the bereaved retreating and hiding from the brutalities of their existence by remaining in the safety zone of their own homes, curtains drawn and curled up in the foetal position in an armchair, sofa or even in bed. They feel accused in the eyes of others while their relationship with the deceased is held up for public scrutiny; they can also experience the attribution of blame intensely and feel exposed and ashamed in their loneliness. In their abandonment they do not care how they look, and rest their exhaustion in the stillness and quietness of a solitary confinement, feeling as if no one has ever felt like this before.

Those grieving may have been left without a single reassurance that they had mattered to the deceased, and often can be seen holding on to something that symbolises the relationship they held with their loved one. Events leading up to the suicide are gone over and over again in an attempt to piece together all the relevant facts that may help to make sense of what has taken place. Thoughts that the dead person may not have had time to prepare for their death through prayer and religious sacraments affect some mourners greatly, and also brings about concerns for their own death and also for the death of those they witness around them.

Many of those grieving now also doubt the existence and presence of a caring God and feel great resentment, asking:

- Why me?
- Why us?
- Why did this have to happen?
- Am I being punished for something done or not done?
- How did I fail?
- Wasn't I loving or caring enough?
- What kind of a loving God gives life only for it to be taken so cruelly?
- What is this life for?
- Could I have done something to prevent the suicide?
- Why wasn't it me who died?

So many similar thoughts are experienced in the early stages of grief following this most denigrating form of rejection. Numbness and a sense of working on automatic pilot takes place, with a shutting down of emotions. All that has been valued and believed is now challenged, a new paradigm imposes itself, and nothing seems to make sense about the world any longer. A sudden unexpected death reprioritises life and there is a sacred humility in never being able to ask 'Why?' The person who chose death over life is no longer present to answer questions or to fall prey to the moral onus.

The bereaved know the ways in which they have failed, and more than any jury they will sentence themselves to the shame of reliving every moment, imagining how they could have changed something to bring about a different outcome. They watch others go on with their lives while feeling they have none to go on with themselves, and they also mourn acutely the loss of many unfulfilled dreams. They fear being a burden on others and not being able to cope. Gradually, with grace, strength and inner integrity, they can overcome the loss, but this process takes time, and while it can't be hurried, it can be greatly assisted by those who offer love, affection, understanding and approval.

Most of us find the act of self-destruction very hard to fully comprehend and death by suicide can have incredible power over the lives of survivors, family, relatives, friends and society at large. Parents have feelings of rage over the selfishness of their child who has taken their own life, children feel abandoned with the loss of security and safety when a parent has chosen death, siblings experience withdrawal and enormous self-blame and guilt when a brother or sister commits suicide, and a surviving spouse struggles alone with numerous difficulties and problems while feeling that they are going insane.

There seems to be a natural reaction from well-intentioned people who wish to comfort the bereaved, to assume a teacher-student posture and to give advice. Such advice can often seem incomprehensible and arrogant to a grieving person, at a time when nothing makes sense and logic isn't even remotely connected to the real nature of their feelings and thinking. In the shock of loss, those bereaved develop finely tuned antenna for picking up platitudes and clichés, which are meant as condolences, but are often perceived as being insults or even self-serving condescendence.

The bereaved become gifted with unbridled, uncensored honesty that grants them the freedom to speak what's on their minds bluntly and openly. Being stripped of all dignity leaves the grieved with little use for façades. Often their tolerance runs out and they can no longer be gracious, and so, acting like wounded animals, they lash out in anger and bitterness at anyone or anything that tries to make meaning out of the nonsensicality of death. Mourning can be a time when the cruellest things are said such as:

- *Time's a great healer!*
  Time alone does not heal and must not be taken for a healer. It only brings a new perspective and when those bereaved are faced with future losses then the hurts resurface to overwhelm them once again.
- *There's a reason for everything.*
  In the minds of those grieving there is no good reason for such devastating pain and loss.
- *God is good.*
  To those grieving a 'good God' wouldn't give only to take away and leave such emptiness.
- *God has deserted you.*
  Having been abandoned and rejected by a person who chose to leave is bad enough, but to also add God as doing the same is far too much for those grieving. God may be a comforting, reassuring presence for many and it's wrong to make such a negative, untrue statement. God never deserts us, especially in an hour of need.
- *Your loved one is at peace now.*
  Those bereaved aren't feeling at peace or at ease and are struggling in their pain, but hopefully they won't have to go

to heaven to find peace again. This statement also implies that the deceased was struggling in their life and couldn't find anyone or anything to ease their difficulties.

- *He/she is up in Heaven with the angels.*
Bereaved people just want the person back on earth amongst them again. It does not help them to hear that their loved one is elsewhere and happy with angels. It implies that he or she wasn't happy with them.

- *God can be so cruel.*
To the bereaved ears this sounds as if God has picked the family out for punishment, which is wrong and very unhelpful. It also implies that a loving, nurturing, sustaining God is only so when He decides to be.

- *How are you feeling?*
The bereaved don't know how they're supposed to be feeling or indeed even what they're feeling. Their emptiness is not in the past, nor in the present, and not yet in the future.

- *How will you cope?*
How on earth can anyone bereaved by a suicide know how they will cope with such a traumatic loss or indeed if they will cope at all? It's as if they are strangers in a new land, without roadways for a guide, and they've lost their way.

- *You must be in a state of shock.*
Those recently bereaved feel that their world has been turned upside down. It's as if they are living in a nightmare and they can't waken up. They don't know if they're in a state of shock and they don't know if they're not in a state of shock. They don't even know if they're in reality. Nothing makes sense and they're totally confused.

- *This is a terrible tragedy.*
Those grieving are left wondering if their loved one's death is a 'tragedy' for the deceased, for themselves or for others.

A tragedy implies a disaster on a large scale and yet the loss is perceived to be a personal one.

- *He or she had everything to live for.*

Well this statement couldn't possibly make sense. If the lost loved one had everything to live for then they'd be alive instead of dead. Obviously the deceased hadn't everything. Something important was missing from their lives to make them want out of it.

- *God never gives us more than we are able to cope with* or *God makes the back for the burden.*

To the bereaved this is a stupid statement, as if it were true then suicides wouldn't take place. Many suicides are undertaken because people become disillusioned, overstressed, depressed, overwhelmed and over-burdened. They can't cope and have no wish to continue on any longer.

- *You're so brave and strong.*

This implies that these qualities are good while weakness and feeble-minded ones are not and the bereaved must have been lacking in strength and bravery.

- *I can't believe he/she would do such a terrible thing.*

This implies that already people see the deceased in a new light. Somehow his/her memory and all that they had been and could have been means nothing anymore. By taking their own lives they are now perceived in a non-living, non-accepting and in a dismissive way. They are no longer held in esteem. This is painful for the bereaved to hear.

- *He/she was not meant for this life.*

If this were true then why was the person born into the family unit? It implies that the person was a misfit from day one and that they were somehow a mistake and mistakes have to be rectified. This is so cruel for the grieved to hear and comprehend.

- *He or she has not gone, they will always be with you.*

For those grieving this means little as they can neither see nor talk with the person. Many feel like killing their loved one for having killed themselves and for leaving so much pain and anguish behind.

- *You're young, you'll get over this.*
  This is not helpful to hear as it minimises the loss experienced and only reinforces the long years ahead without the loved one's presence.

- *No one knows what's around the corner.*
  This statement causes panic in those grieving. They ask what more could happen out of the blue. They begin to watch other family members closely, in case they too would take their own lives.

- *I know how you feel.*
  How can anyone ever know how someone else feels? Do they walk in the other person's shoes, feel the same emotions, have the same experiences and dream the same dreams?

- *You'll look back and remember the good times.*
  In the early stages of grief all the wonderful memories of the lost loved one are with them. The bereaved can't perceive of a future without the deceased and so this statement really doesn't make sense to them.

- *You must do this or you must do that.*
  The bereaved have little energy and do what they feel they are capable of at any given time. To be told that they must do this or that only causes alarm and panic in them, as they often are just capable of breathing.

So often in the days following a suicide it isn't the actual loss that makes the bereaved feel insane but rather it's the way that others treat them.

While a conventional expression of sympathy can't be avoided, it is better to offer it quietly, saying 'I'm sorry for your troubles', or 'I'm sorry for your loss', and then to speak from the heart, avoiding clichés and taking cues from the bereaved themselves. Talking about trivialities is irrelevant at such a time, and this makes conversations somewhat difficult, so it's best to say little on an early visit and to be aware of the need to use a different approach depending on the person's age, sex, relationship to the deceased and their emotional state at the time. It is much easier for helpers to take in personal styles when those grieving are known to them. Dealing with strangers is more difficult as there is no prior knowledge about particular characteristics. What is seen is what has to be dealt with. This requires considerable flexibility, in knowing how best to focus on the dead person rather than on the act of death itself, and in permitting freedom of expression. Crying and talking brings thoughts and feelings to the surface and releases them.

In being sensitive to what's being said, helpers become aware of the pain, discomfort and social stigma of suicide. They also become aware of the reactions and emotions of others who are close, and of life partners, as well as their own unique reactions. In accepting whatever feelings are expressed it is important not to change the subject or to rebuke in any way, while being as genuine and understanding as possible. One cannot know how the bereaved is feeling, but one can learn from the mourner. It is important not to instruct or to probe for details about the death and to show by a willingness to reveal ones own feelings that helpers are not ashamed or destroyed by them. Such sharing fosters a mutual respect that is productive, open, trusting and hope-inspiring.

Those bereaved by suicide are strongly affected by the views and actions of relevant other people and are constantly comparing their beliefs with others. They fear being judged harshly, rejected or even disliked, and have a longing to be both accepted and acceptable. Helpers can guide those bereaved in their attempts to feel 'normal', 'accepted', and 'right' by their quiet presence and acknowledgement of their value and loss, and through their tribute to the dead, through gentle communication of affectionate understanding via a touch on a shoulder or a squeeze of a hand, or by just sitting composed in accepted silences. By having the patience to allow repetition, a clear message is given to the bereaved that they are not alone, that they are understood, valued, worthwhile and cared for. The outcome of this experience is very therapeutic for the bereaved in that they feel much better at having released built-up tensions and experienced emotional arousal. They become aware of their thoughts and feelings, having been able to tell their story without detecting critical judgement from the listener, and as a result they feel less shame and more self-acceptance. They also feel closer to the person that they have spoken with.

Helpers are a life-line for the bereaved

Friends: With practical experience they can fill the routine needs for meals, sandwiches and tea. They can answer the door, take telephone messages and generally help with enquiries. When children are involved, such friends can deal with bath times, bedtime stories and general childcare activities. They can also be a strong, protective and comforting source for the grieving family as a whole.

Schools and Teachers: They can provide much needed support by preparing class friends for the return of the bereaved child. They can sensitively explain the death and arrange attendance at the funeral. Special prayers of remembrance in assembly can be said and, very importantly, a watch kept for bereavement bullying.

Clergy: They are in a very privileged position in their roles to give help, advice and comfort to those grieving. They can demonstrate by their manner an acceptance of the grief reaction, and particularly acceptance of the bitter anger against God that may be expressed. Often those grieving following a suicide no longer feel that they know how to react to the clergy, but they long for understanding and acceptance and may even see the clergy as being the representatives of Jesus and thus a loving parent figure, one who is strong, understanding and a source of love. Clergy may not be able to bring back the dead person or make everything right again, and nor can they give all the answers, but they can bring some meaning by saying just the right prayers or by quoting the right biblical quotation. Parishioners who know their clergy will be far more likely to accept them than those who are complete strangers. All clergy, however, are often perceived as being a 'life-line' for those in distress. They can be trusted and believed as being a credible source of information. Being able to speak in confidence allows for the release of emotions and fosters beneficial healing. It also brings the reality of the death circumstances out in the open. Clergy, in their compassion and sensitivity, demonstrate that in all problems it is important to be aware of God's presence, leading, supporting and strengthening us along the way, and in speaking with authenticity e.g. 'You are never alone' or 'You will be guided from a higher source', they make simple explanations reverberate with enormous truths.

In grief, some people cannot hear what is being said to them, and others cannot hear what they want to hear, so it's very much appreciated when clergy use flexibility in making funeral arrangements and in the writing of a homily. Funerals can be an ordeal, but they demonstrate that people are willing to spare the time to show their respects to the dead and to the family. Rituals and a burial make the death into a reality, and the bereaved appreciate being given a copy of the homily so that they can read comforting and uplifting words at a later date. Once the funeral is over, and the loved one is put to rest, the bereaved face a tough and lonely road in coming to terms with their loss.

Flowers, condolences cards, poems, letters, prayers and other symbols of comfort and kind thought are received with heartfelt thanks, and remind those in grief that while death teaches aloneness, there can also be togetherness in being alone. A suicide is not a personal vendetta against anyone but rather it is a response to a profound spiritual dilemma. It takes a long time to respect the factors of mystery in our spiritual lives and even longer to become comfortable in living with unknowns. It is possible to find meaning in life again, but such an experience does change individuals. They see as never before the pursuits that are trivial and the institutions that pigeonhole them into roles that they do not want. Gradually the flow of pain is turned back, healing takes place, and those who have been so tragically bereaved move on to a life full and serene and ever thankful for those helping hands and touches.

CHAPTER THREE

My Survival Struggle

THE EXPERIENCE of my husband's suicide left me shocked and directionless. It seemed as if I had been tossed into stormy seas without even a life-jacket to keep me afloat. My world became filled with uncertainty, problems, pain and loss. I felt emotionally and physically battered and no longer grounded or centred. Past issues, stresses and problems associated with my husband could not be dealt with and this proved to be a very difficult and painful legacy. My world became hostile, unpredictable and unstable. My sense of trust had been broken and I felt rejection in the most hurtful of ways. My perceptions of everyone and everything changed and that included how I viewed myself – I felt changed forever.

Throughout my grieving process my emotions and feelings were all jumbled up and included the following:

A

ABSENT-MINDEDNESS: Thoughts of my late husband and of his action of suicide became so distracting that I became very absent-minded and, as a result, accident-prone. I honestly became a danger to myself and to others around me. Such absent-mindedness added greatly to the feelings of going crazy and mad.

ACCEPTANCE: As time passes healing really does take place, and no matter how much despair and anguish is experienced it is possible to go beyond fear and loss in order to recognise life in a new and a meaningful way. It required honesty and openness, and a long period before I felt reasonably normal again, but there is always life after sorrow.

ALIENATION: My reactions to everyone and everything became a little deadened. I had very little energy to either hear or perceive emotional support. The sense of alienation added to the feelings of being utterly and unbearably crushed.

ANGER: While anger may be considered a normal part of the grief reaction, I felt it to be intensified in a number of ways – anger at God, at the world, at professionals, at friends, at family members, at myself and also at my late husband for daring to take his own life. To me it seemed as if my late husband had left behind an imprint of anger on everyone.

ANXIETY: Anxiety and fears were very much part of my grieving. At best they could be described as being uncomfortable experiences that gradually faded. The signs and symptoms of the anxiety that I experienced were:

- Rapid heart beats
- Palpitations
- Loss of appetite
- An inability to relax
- A dry mouth
- Sweaty palms

- A constriction in the throat
- Abdominal cramps
- Diarrhoea
- Dizziness
- A ringing in the ears
- Headaches
- Yawning
- Excessive sweating
- Feelings of insecurity
- Nightmares
- Poor concentration
- Poor memory
- Irritability
- Health and death concerns

B

BEREAVEMENT PROCESS: While the bereavement process is important in enabling people to come to terms with and to adapt to their tragic loss, I found grieving very hard work indeed, and being an active process it required a great deal of my already depleted energy reserves.

BLAME: The attribution of blame for my husband's suicide by my in-laws drove a wedge into family relationships. Instead of bringing people together, such active blame brought active avoidance, hostility, accusations and ostracism. I also blamed myself for not having done enough to prevent my husband's death.

BRAVE FACE: Often I would be feeling utterly distraught, numbed and drained, but I'd put on a brave face and just get on with things. Inwardly I was finding it hard to take in that my husband really had died and wouldn't be coming back.

C

CONCENTRATION: My mind was confused, overwhelmed and overloaded. It shifted so much that I found it hard to focus or hold onto thoughts. It required enormous effort on my part to concentrate for any length of time.

CONFRONTATIONS: As much as I wished to I couldn't confront my late husband and ask why it was necessary for him to take his own life and in so doing leave behind so much pain and suffering. The need in me to confront those who could have offered help to my husband and didn't was overwhelming. I longed to be heard, but was concerned with speaking out in pain without thought or consideration, so I preferred to keep myself to myself until such a time when confrontation no longer seemed pressing.

CONTEMPLATION: Sitting quietly and daydreaming was good for both my mind and body. Often I was 'not really with it' and thoughts were not focused on my immediate surroundings. Preoccupation with my late husband removed me to a different level of functioning and I found that questions and requests had to be repeated before they finally registered with me.

COPING: The overwhelming shock and sense of loss left me under par, with little reserves of energy for dealing with the many tasks involved following a death from suicide. I felt unable to cope with even the simplest of mundane tasks and I found this to be very upsetting.

CRY FOR HELP: Suicide has been called the 'ultimate cry for help', but I felt that it was my husband's final rejection of us and in that sense it was the 'ultimate cry of anger'. By leaving us to live with pain, confusion and guilt, his suicide was a form of manipulation.

CRYING: Crying is a safety value for emotional pressure and at times an uncomfortable urge to weep and cry out loud in anguish used to rise to the surface. Trying not to cry in front of others only made it worse. Weeping and crying was very therapeutic and I found the shower to be a perfect place for the soothing of my mind and body with warm water. Tears should flow but, as in all things, there had to be a balance.

D

DECISION-MAKING: I found that decision-making was nearly impossible for me. My lack of focus and ability to concentrate, as well as a lack of self-esteem, self-confidence and a shaky judgement, all contributed to my indecision.

DEFEATED BY LIFE: The experience of my husband's suicide, the leading up to it and it's aftermath, all added to an overall feeling of being overwhelmed and defeated by life. It was as if I was struggling to overcome a life that I did not want to live and experiences that I did not want to experience. I wanted life to be simple and trouble-free, not one of constant struggling against all the odds.

DEPRESSION: I experienced 'pangs of depression', which included feelings of intense pain, loneliness, hopelessness, lack of hope and joy. The signs and symptoms of my depression included the following:

• Being inward looking
• Distorted perceptions

- Feeling life would always be painful
- Early morning wakening
- Dreading the early hours of the day
- A general lack of interest
- Loss of appetite
- Loss of weight
- Insomnia
- Feelings of unworthiness
- Feelings of futility
- Poor concentration
- Poor memory
- Preoccupation with death
- Suicidal thoughts
- Feeling unable to cope
- Anxiety
- Oversleeping
- Sweating
- Trembling
- Disturbed dreams
- Thumping heart
- Stomach upsets
- Aches and pains
- Self-doubt
- Loss of confidence
- Feelings of inadequacy
- Why bother?
- What's the point of it all?
- Overwhelming feeling of separation, loss and change

DESPAIRING: My husband was gone from his despairing, but he had left behind despairing in his loved ones. The worst way for people to leave us unfairly is to take their own lives and leave us alone. The suicidee decides to die in spite of how much they are needed to remain alive. I knew that I couldn't bring him back and make everything all right. As time progressed I found the use of humour was the best protection against despair.

DIGNITY: It required great dignity and courage for me to deal with all the mourners and well-wishers that offered condolences. All I wanted to do was to be able to turn the clock back and have my husband back with us once again. The funeral and burial were such ordeals that in order to withstand them I felt as if a cloak of dignity was wrapped around me. It also took a great deal of courage and dignity in order for me to be able to face the long lonely days without my husband being alive, and adaptation to such a situation took me a long time.

DISBELIEF: It was very difficult for me to fully realise that my husband's suicide really had taken place. Questions like 'Are you sure?', 'How could this happen?' and 'Was this an accident?' featured strongly. The sense of disbelief prevailed for some time.

DOUBTS: I doubted everything. I was plagued by doubts about my ability to cope, survive, heal and to go on living without the deceased. Doubts about being accepted by others, and concerns over the role I would have to play in the future, also clouded my ability to trust my judgement.

E

EMBARRASSMENT: The embarrassment that is associated with a suicide took many forms. The family felt embarrassed by the stigma involved and the feelings of failure that ensued. Would-be helpers felt embarrassed at attempts to offer condolences, and I felt embarrassed when meeting people for the first time and having to explain the circumstances of my husband's death. I then would have to witness the shock, horror and sorrow that registered on their faces as they struggled to overcome their own embarrassment.

ENCOURAGEMENT: The fact that I was given so much encouragement from family and friends in the early stages of my grief enabled me to progress through the bereavement process and have a successful outcome.

EXPLANATIONS: Having everything explained in plain, easy to understand language helped me to accept the meaning and reality of my situation. Explanations needed to be given more than once and people had to question me to make sure that what had been said was fully understood. I was unable to take in too much information at once so it was good to have explanations broken down into small, more manageable chunks. Patience on behalf of others when dealing with me was a great bonus!

F

FORGIVENESS: In forgiving, we heal the pains that we experience. I had to forgive and excuse when I realised that my husband was not to blame and nor was anyone else. There had to be extenuating circumstances for such a death to happen. It was hard to forgive a husband who could no longer be touched or seen and it was hardest of all to forgive myself. Forgiving enabled me to live again and to realise that no one needs to be perfect, we can only do our best. Forgiving also prevents the deceased from having power over the present as well as the future. Forgiving takes great courage.

FRUSTRATIONS: I had my own particular frustrations and levels of tolerance. In grief everything became more exaggerated and my reactions tended to be hypersensitive, so it was important for me to keep levels of frustration to a minimum. Help in dealing with bureaucracy and various form filling were of enormous benefit and greatly reduced my tendency to become overwhelmed and overburdened.

FUTILITY: I had a vague, nagging feeling that it wasn't possible to feel such pain and live. I wanted to be alone. I felt that no one could help me as I struggled with the painful thoughts and memories that left me frightened and confused. Life for me would never be the same again. My eyes were dim with helplessness and hopelessness. I was merely attempting to exist at this stage, while wondering what was the point of everything. Love and tenderness can make all the difference in lifting such burdensome thoughts.

G

GAINING KNOWLEDGE: While searching brought great insight and understanding, the gaining of knowledge through experience was far more meaningful and insightful than anything learnt from books. I definitely had been strengthened in the school of life and will not view anything in exactly the same way again. I tend now to function at a different level from others and this can lead to slight feelings of separation and loneliness.

GOING MAD: I certainly was overwhelmed by a mixture of painful emotions and terror. I felt vulnerable and isolated with a low satisfaction of life and felt as if my world was crumbling around me. With such intentions it was no wonder that at times I felt as if I were losing my mind and going mad. I soon learnt that these feelings were a natural part of a very difficult grieving process.

GRIEF REACTIONS: Grief following a suicide can take much longer than an uncomplicated grief. Due to the stigma associated with this mode of death, and the fact that the relationship held with the deceased is unique, so the pain of such loss must also be unique to those left behind. It must also encompass the special circumstances surrounding the death.

GUILT: I examined myself for my part in my husband's death and felt guilt, responsibility and self-blame as a result. The guilt I experienced prolonged my recovery and came from a feeling of regret or remorse at having either done or not done something that could have prevented such a tragic act. I went over every argument, every conversation and felt that I should be punished like someone who had committed some crime. I had accused myself falsely and had to strive to prevent such inner judgement from making me feel sorry for being alive when my husband was dead.

H

HALF ALIVE/HALF DEAD: In my struggle to come to terms with and to adapt to my loss, I felt as if part of me was missing. The remaining part of myself had to struggle and cope while longing to be reunited with that part of me that was gone. I worked on automatic pilot and carried out actions routinely while my thoughts were taken up with the deceased.

HATE: Hate is the instinctive reaction against anyone who wounds us wrongly, and following my husband's suicide I had to hate someone I also loved. Hate robbed me of my energy and it needed to be healed. Hating the action of the suicide and not the suicidee was somewhat difficult, but it was vital to free the deceased from the hurt that they had caused. Hurt, when not attended to, only grows and festers until it stifles all joy. My wounds may have looked superficial to others, but I knew differently. I had to remember that my late husband was weak, needy and a fallible human being – as we all are.

HEALING AND TRANSFORMATION: When my grieving process had been travelled through, healing did take place. The pain of loss subsided and was integrated, leaving me feeling transformed. I have become independent of the good or bad opinion of others. I recognise that I am beneath or above no one and can be fearless in the face of any challenge.

HELPLESSNESS: When a tragedy such as suicide occurs, everyone experiences a sense of hopelessness. There was nothing I or anyone else could do to make things better and bring the deceased back, and this reinforced our feelings of limitations.

HURT: Missing my husband hurt and took the form of sadness, depression, low spirits, anger and emptiness. Bodily sensations due to such hurt included tense muscles, headaches and back pain. My husband did not have to act as he did and I will always be left with this knowledge and the mysteries surrounding such a loss.

I

INDEPENDENCE: I wanted my basic needs met, especially when I was hurting, but independence was important for becoming my own person. I had to cultivate my abilities to stand on my own and not to become too dependent upon others for a sense of well-being. Independence fostered an inner equilibrium and an ability to face difficulties. The future is a territory of the unknown, but with an inner strength and a power of reserve it can be faced with confidence and joy.

INNER GLOW: At times a warm wave of comfort flowed throughout the whole of my body. It was very pleasing and a welcoming, comforting sensation that brought a warm glow to my skin – like a flush of hope. In the midst of all the negative feelings and experiences it was a welcomed, soothing reminder that healing was a possibility and that I could experience joy again.

INSECURITIES: The world was no longer a safe, secure place to be in. It was threatening, unstable and unpredictable. Death by suicide left me physically, emotionally and spiritually insecure. Some of the insurance companies invalidated policies following my husband's mode of death and this only added to financial insecurity for the children and myself.

J

JOY: I found moments of joy even in the toughest of grief reactions. Joy at a sunset, at a sensitive gesture, at smiles, at warm handshakes and joy at being able to feel hopeful again.

K

KINDNESS: By treating myself as I would a close friend or a loved one I was actually acknowledging the fact that I had been dealt a terrible blow that left me reeling with sadness and loss. In not judging myself too harshly I was giving unconditional love to myself. By speaking gently to myself, and never blaming or being harsh or abrasive, I was accepting my limitations in doing the best possible under daunting circumstances. In being kind to myself I invited others to treat me in the same fashion.

L

LAUGHTER: As my grieving eased l[...]
begin with it felt as if I were bei[...]
humour again. Laughter brought a ve[...]
tensions that had built up in my min[...]
uplifted my mood, and endorphins floo[...]
sense of well-being.

LETTING GO: Learning to release my late husband didn't mean completely erasing the memories. It involved my letting go of expectations for the relationship and future. I began to recall my husband with special forgiveness and understanding. I was confident in the knowledge that he was at peace. I let go of someone who no longer needed me.

LIFE AFTER SUICIDE: I found the bereavement process to be a lengthy one and a tough and lonely road. It was possible to find meaning in life again, but my experiences through doing so have changed me forever. I have had to pick myself up and learn important lessons. I now speak out whenever someone or something is wrong. I am no different from other people except for the fact that I have had to call upon inborn abilities, which, in fact, everyone possesses.

LOVE: Self-love brought me to a quiet place within in the midst of all the chaos going on around me. It allowed me to pass through the stages of bereavement at my own pace. The love I experienced from our animals, and extended family and friends, brought warmth, compassion recognition, understanding, approval, and an acceptance of my individual strengths and weaknesses. All love stems from a higher part of ourselves.

M

MINDS: Never knowing what went on in my husband's mind meant that I had somehow to resolve my loss without ever knowing what he was either thinking or feeling before he chose death over life.

MISUNDERSTOOD: I found it difficult enough to understand myself so it came as no surprise that others couldn't understand me either. Slowness and indecision, tears and a preoccupation with the deceased as well as feelings of futility and ongoing anger tended to produce impatience in others. Would-be helpers learnt to make allowances for confusion that arose from misunderstandings and in so doing, prevented the reinforcement of even more confusion in me.

N

NEGATIVITY: The outlook seemed negative to me, as I had felt that, in some way, I had failed and was not a good person. It seemed as if nothing good would ever come about again and the world seemed grey to me. Continued negativity only led me to feel depressed so I had to learn to change my thinking and outlook. Healing began when I shifted negative thoughts for more positive ones.

NIGHTMARES: When I was relaxed in sleep my conscious mind went off duty and all the unresolved material that lay buried surfaced. When it became too threatening I'd awaken at once with a feeling of great relief. The disconcerting effects of these nightmares often lasted into the day and I dreaded going to sleep and experiencing them all again.

NO CONTROL: Having no control over events brought feelings of helplessness, mental confusion and emotional upheaval. Along with the loss of my husband came a sense of vanishing security, feelings of uncertainty, inadequacy, and loss of self-esteem, and any confidence that I may have possessed.

NUISANCE: Feeling like a nuisance to others was a direct result of feeling vulnerable, uncertain and undeserving. Low self-esteem and self-worth coupled with other negative feelings left me feeling as if I were a burden and an annoyance to others. I struggled in my depression and lack of coping, and relied upon others for help and support, yet I found the asking for help very difficult when it was most needed.

NUMB: My experience of numbness was due to both the shock at such a sudden death as well as the overwhelming emotions that I experienced. I believe that this numbness is mother natures' way of protection from too much strain. Numbness allowed me to carry out the necessary tasks for coping with the immediate aftermath of my husband's suicide.

O

ONE DAY AT A TIME: Just getting through one day was an enormous effort on my part. I was so thankful to have another day over. On wakening I used to feel a hollow at the pit of my stomach at the prospect of having to face yet another day. Worries and concerns were just about manageable on a daily basis, but could become too threatening if I dwelt on long days and nights without my husband. 'Don't worry about tomorrow, let the future take care of itself' was a very relevant statement and wise advice when I struggled with emotional deprivation.

OVERCOMING GRIEF: While there may be no right or wrong way to grieve the suicide of a loved one, it is important that all strong emotions should be expressed as opposed to being kept hidden. Unresolved grief led to long term effects on my health, happiness and well-being. Once I allowed myself to express my grief openly then my health and well-being improved.

OVERLOADING: As my energies were so depleted, it was important to take as much rest as was possible. Taking on new responsibilities only taxed my already weakened reserves and led to my body and mind becoming overloaded. Too much stress would have led to burn-out, so I learnt to delegate when opportunities presented themselves. My body, like a machine, was finally tuned and gave out warnings that too many demands were being made on it.

P

PAIN: My pain seemed unjust, unfair and unnecessary and threw me into crisis. I tried to deny my pain because of my pride and also because it hurt too much to acknowledge it. The pain was deep and persuasive and it presented itself in anger and hostility, while the anticipation of such pain caused me great anxiety. Pain that I turned inwards created even more guilt and depression. I found that the letting go of pain was not easy and found release by firing stones into water, by walking briskly or by watching balloons floating away while symbolically taking my pain away with them.

PANICS AND ALARM: Panic attacks came on suddenly and were very distressing. It felt as if I had no power over my mind or body. The feeling of such insecurity made me long to stay at home and avoid any embarrassment that may be caused by my losing control. As I had to go out and do many necessary tasks for the children I prevented a vicious circle that could have led to me becoming evermore isolated, insecure and fearful. Panic attacks occurred when anxiety and fear were extreme and the symptoms included:

- Dizziness
- Shortness of breath
- Difficulty in breathing
- Nausea
- Trembling
- Sweating
- Fainting
- Palpitations
- Desire for the bathroom
- Feelings of unreality
- Tingly sensations
- Light-headedness
- Hot flushes
- Chest pain
- Fear of dying
- Blurred vision
- Fear of going mad
- Fear of losing control
- Tense, tight muscles

My panic attacks were short lived and were followed by exhaustion and a dread that they would occur again. As time passed these attacks became less and less until they vanished as quickly as they had appeared.

PASSIVENESS: While I may have appeared to be passive in my behaviour, which was slowed down so much that most of the time I could be found either sitting or lying down, my grieving was an active process with a lot going on inside of myself.

PAST TIMES: While the past couldn't be changed, I could change how I viewed it. I focused on the good times and thought of my husband's death as being a life completed instead of being cut short. Changing my perceptions enabled me to live in the present while looking forward to a brighter future.

PATIENCE: I wanted to ask for instant healing, but my healing came very slowly. Often it seemed as if it were one step forward and several backwards. There were days when everything went well and others when all was wrong. Gaining patience allowed me to 'go with the flow' and 'weather the storm' and wait until joy could be experienced again, when the sun would shine and lightness would be all around.

PEACE: A feeling of peace and calm flooded my body at various times throughout my grieving and it was such a welcome respite from the unsettled, restless feeling that usually predominated. Relaxation and walks along beaches gave me wonderful peace and serenity and made my life more bearable.

PHYSICAL MANIFESTATIONS: Bereavement brought many physical changes in my body including:

- Headaches
- Nausea
- Cramps and diarrhoea
- Dry mouth
- Poor co-ordination
- An inability to remain still
- Accident proneness
- A pounding heart rate
- Tiredness
- Sleep disturbances
- Flu-like symptoms
- Upset stomach

- Inability to focus eyes properly
- Backache
- Fast breathing
- Raised blood pressure
- Searching
- Panic attacks
- Fainting
- General weakness
- Wobbly like a jelly
- Exhaustion

PINING: Pining for my husband involved a lot of sitting and staring into space while half expecting him to turn up at any moment. It involved looking at his photograph and twisting my wedding and engagement rings around my finger.

PREPARATION: I was unable to prepare myself for the shock, stress, pain, loss and feelings of rejection that followed my husband's suicide. All of my questions as to why he chose death over life were unanswered. The pain I experienced was inescapable and persuasive, leaving every part of me crying out for answers.

PRIVACY: Privacy was essential for me in order to collect my thoughts and recharge my batteries. It afforded me respite from the society of others. Quiet moments of privacy throughout the day enabled the rejuvenation and regeneration of my mind, body and spirit. It enabled me to become more centred and stable while preventing overloading by stressful stimuli.

PROBLEMS IN GRIEF: I seemed to have so many problems that I wondered if I were still on planet earth. The following reflected numerous concerns for me as a young bereaved mother:

- Emotional and physical concerns
- Financial concerns
- Waiting for monies to be released
- A long, intense bereavement
- Waiting for the inquest
- Feeling pressured
- Feeling 'I should be over it by now'
- Easy, roll off the tongue platitudes
- Being forced to eat
- Being forced to be sociable
- Having to put on a brave face
- Meeting new people
- Having to explain the circumstances of my husband's death
- Watching others reactions
- Celebrations, anniversaries
- Never knowing what was on other people's minds
- Never having answers to questions
- Unfinished business
- Becoming stuck in grief
- Guilt
- Feeling unsupported and undervalued
- Feeling uncared for and unloved
- Remembrances
- Extra demands
- Attribution of blame
- Negative memories

PUTTING AFFAIRS INTO ORDER: Being left to pick up the pieces following my husband's suicide left me with the feeling that absolutely nothing is predictable or secure in this world. There was so much paper work to do, organisations to deal with and preparations to undertake that I felt an overwhelming urge to put my own affairs into order before facing my own death. I made my will with careful, detailed instructions and I had all relevant papers put into order. When all was completed to my satisfaction I relaxed a little.

R

RELAXATION AND MEDITATION: I found that when my body was relaxed then so was my mind. In taking the time to relax and mediate, I was able to see a tiny bit of improvement daily. Closing windows, locking doors, sitting or lying down covered by a blanket created the right atmosphere for such relaxation. It allowed my mind to just drift away into a dream-like state. Relaxation and meditation on calming images helped to give me more control over my emotions.

RELIEF: There had been so much discord and unpleasantness in my relationship with my late husband that I experienced a tremendous sense of relief at being able to live without the fear of his threats of harm or suicide. I also felt relief for my husband who found peace in being released from all his own troubles and turmoil.

RELIGIOUS BELIEFS: A belief in a Higher source provided an enormous substance for me by bring some order, purpose and meaning to life. It enabled me to become more outward looking and in so doing prevented me from being completely destroyed. It encouraged the letting go of my husband in love and caring, and encouraged me to begin again as healing took place. It reassured me that one day I'd be reunited with loved ones departed and it helped me make some sense of all that had taken place. My life did change by the direct result of knowing God, and in a more direct and personal way.

RELIVING EVENTS: I went over and over the events leading up to the suicide. I tortured myself with what I could have done to prevent it. I had, after all, picked up the signals and clues so I should have tried harder to save him. I felt that I had failed my husband as he made the choice of death over life.

S

SADNESS: The sadness that I experienced was a profound one. I felt sadness at the senselessness of the suicide act, at the choices my husband made, at never knowing why we weren't enough for him, at not having prevented the death, at never seeing my husband again, but mostly I was saddened at the loss of a life never to be again.

SELF-CONSCIOUSNESS: I felt that the eyes of the world were upon me. I felt as if I were watched and judged harshly. I felt changed and also tainted by my husband's mode of death. I became very sensitive and very self-conscious.

SELF-RESPECT: Self pep talks helped to ease my feelings of futility and inadequacy. Self-respect came from knowing that I did the best possible under very difficult circumstances. It came from holding my head high and being the very best that I could be. It involved taking care of myself and thinking that I could survive loss and complete tasks and demands in my own time and in my own way. I had to realise that I was indeed a worthwhile, vulnerable human who had a right to continue on with my own life.

SENSES: I found that all of my senses were heightened in my grieving. Sight, hearing, touch, smell and taste were all greatly exaggerated in sensitivity and that left me very easily irritated. Thoughts of my loss left little energy for anything else and the slightest request for information or action left me irritated and annoyed.

SHAME: Feelings of shame came from within myself and also from without. I felt shame at being implicated in my husband's death, at my husband's decision to opt out from all of his responsibilities and promises, and shame at how others would perceive me. I longed to hide away from the wider world in my shame.

SHARING FEELINGS: I found the sharing of my true feelings concerning my late husband rather difficult as others did not see him in exactly the same way. Others were shocked to hear that there were aspects of my husband that they were ignorant of. Speaking ill of the dead is considered to be in bad taste, so sharing negative feelings with others was nearly impossible for me. Sharing my emotions and experiences with others who were not directly involved with my husband proved to be an enormous relief.

SLEEP DISTURBANCES: I experienced a regular disturbance of my sleep pattern. In the early hours of the morning there was wakefulness and remaining awake for a long time, only managing to fall asleep again when it was time to get up. Everything seemed worse at night time and I found myself prey to the torments of many joyless, troubling thoughts and fears.

SOCIAL ATTITUDES: I feel that while ways of responding to death by suicide have changed radically, society is still somewhat uneasy with matters surrounding such a death. Society provokes responses from the public that can be either nonchalant or unconcerned, and in grief I felt that my social standing had somewhat deteriorated.

SPECIAL AND SPECIFIC GROUP SUPPORT: I found that speaking with individuals or with groups of people who have lost a loved one to suicide really did help. It allowed for honest expression of feelings and concerns in an atmosphere of support, non-judgment and non-rejection. It also provided social opportunities in the early stages of bereavement to see others who had survived and come through their loss while remaining sensitive to the needs of others. Socialising with survivors also allowed for repetition and endless going over of events while unravelling some very complex and difficult thoughts. Reassurances were also given that I wasn't going mad and all that I was experiencing was normal.

STAGES OF GRIEF: My grief followed a predictable pattern of stages, such as shock, denial, anger, and acceptance, which merged until my grieving was completed. The first part lasted several days when a feeling of numbness and an unwillingness to accept the fact of death occurred. The second part lasted for six months and involved experiencing extreme sadness, overwhelming waves of guilt, bouts of crying, sleep disturbances and a preoccupation with my late husband. The third part brought an ease and a gradual returning to everyday life and involvement once again.

STRESS: The biggest single cause of stress is the death of a loved one by suicide. The loss combined with the disruption in routines dealt a severe emotional blow for me. The stress response that I experienced followed a definite pattern. Firstly there was the experience of alarm, followed by resistance and an attempt at adaptation, and finally an equilibrium or an exhaustion occurred. My body's response to stress included:

- A knot in my stomach
- Coldness
- Sweaty palms
- Goose pimples

- Crying
- A dry mouth
- Vomiting
- Indigestion
- Tight muscles
- Yawning
- Watery eyes
- Restlessness
- Speechlessness at times
- Mental blocks
- Confusion
- Anxiousness
- Forgetfulness
- Feeling a sense of impending doom
- Feelings of being out of control
- Missing the point

Recognising that I was actually stressed enough to do something about it, I managed my stress levels by doing the following:

- Gentle stretching exercises
- Slowing down my thinking
- Rest and sleep
- Eating a balanced diet
- Learning to say 'no' to demands
- Slowing down my actions
- Releasing bottled up emotions
- Not drinking or smoking
- Not masking any problems
- Deep breathing and relaxation
- Exercising
- Knowing my strengths and also my limitations and weaknesses

- Taking time out
- Facing fears
- Taking control of my life
- Asking for help
- Delegating chores and certain responsibilities
- Listening to soothing music
- Positive thinking
- Involvement in enjoyable and calming activities.

SURVIVAL: The word 'survive' comes from the Latin words *supe*, which means 'over', and *vivere*, to 'live'. It is a good word to use in describing my struggle for overcoming my husband's suicide. My bereavement process was both prolonged and severe and I realised that I had a right to survive and that my husband would have wanted me to survive also.

SYMPATHY: Feeling the sympathy of friends enabled me to feel that I wasn't totally alone. It greatly eased my overall feelings of isolation and loneliness. Sympathy is an emotion for which I will always be grateful.

T

TOUCH: Hugs and handshakes spoke a thousand words and gave the warmth of human kindness. I found touch to be a gentle form for the communication of affectionate understanding and it made me feel worthwhile and cared for. It greatly reinforced in me the sense that I wasn't really on my own.

U

UNDERSTANDING: The more understanding I had, the easier the journey was towards wholeness and happiness. The quality of my life came from within myself, and all pain, hurt and fears were finally dissolved. A few precious moments of understanding can repair a lifetime of ignorance.

UNFINISHED BUSINESS: Unfinished business refers to any problems or difficulties within the relationship that were not dealt with prior to the death. The finality of death means that the resolution of such problems cannot now take place and I had to find ways of accepting this. I wrote a letter to my late husband saying all that needed to be said and releasing him into God's care. This letter contained all the sadness, frustrations, resentments, loneliness, regrets and love that I felt. I then ceremonially burnt the letter and found that I could then move on with my grief.

UNLOVED: Rejection by my husband's suicide left me feeling as if the children and myself had never mattered to him. My reasoning was that had he cared enough he wouldn't have caused us so much pain and the struggling with so many mixed emotions and unsolved issues. The experience of such cruel rejection left me shut off from experiencing all the warmth and loving care that was surrounding me.

UNREALITY: Time stood still and a change in my perceptions came with the passing of time. I found it to be a real effort just to calculate the day of the week, as nothing seemed to either look or feel the same anymore. A sense of change prevailed and what was taking place seemed false and artificial.

V

VALUE IN LIFE AGAIN: Life is very sacred so it's important to enjoy every moment of it. My husband's suicide enabled me to grow and develop into the person that I am today. The darkness that was experienced has been replaced by a light that has filled

well as healing my broken heart. This light is
of healing. I now look forward to the future
er, wiser and more aware, with a compassion
...nding for those experiencing difficult times. I have
...veloped and matured and no longer feel so tense, anxious,
guilty, angry, depressed or hostile. I have moved on to leave
behind the role of helpless victim and have transformed my life
with vitality and energy. Embracing life once more includes
being thankful for even the simplest of things, including being
thankful for the loved one lost to me.

What helped in my struggle for survival:

- Optimism
- Love
- Acceptance
- Kindness
- Peace
- Quiet times
- Classical music
- Poetry
- Meditation
- Beauty
- Breathing in love and exhaling fear
- Beaches
- Knowing I had a home beyond this planet
- Avoiding extra stresses
- Asking for help
- Letting emotions and feelings flow
- Being kind and gentle on myself
- Taking time to just sit and be
- Not setting too many goals
- Having patience with myself and everyone

My Survival Struggle

- Reducing frustrations
- Conserving energies
- Preventing overloading
- Taking one day at a time
- Hugs and kisses
- Warm handshakes
- Smiles
- Animals
- Friends
- Routines
- Genuine offers of help
- Explanations and choices
- Having meals prepared for us
- Help around the house
- Help with messages
- Fresh air
- Gentle exercises
- Being listened to
- Doing things at my own pace
- Self-discipline
- Gaining knowledge
- Keeping a light and radio on for background comfort
- Reassurances and encouragement
- Relaxation and mediation
- Sensitive touches
- Rest
- Privacy
- Laughter
- Time for healing
- Self pep talks
- Self-praising
- Becoming involved in something
- Being accepted

my grieving

- ilms
- books
- soothing, relaxing music
- Meditation and prayer
- Being amongst others bereaved by suicide
- Seeing others who had survived
- Weathering the storm
- Breaking down tasks
- Faith in a higher source
- Endurance abilities
- Acceptance, patience and understanding
- Grief counselling with specially trained counsellors
- Being able to leave social gatherings when I wanted to
- Forgiving
- Viewing the body
- A good solicitor
- Coping and dealing with unfinished business
- Receiving and giving
- Self-respect
- A caring clergyman

What didn't help in my grieving:

- All the legal work
- Form filling
- Waiting for the post mortem
- Waiting for monies to be released
- Never having time for myself
- Feeling 'I should be over it'
- The long bereavement process

My Survival Struggle

- Difficult funeral and burial service
- Being the focus for the attribution of b
- People speaking ill of my late husband
- People saying 'it's for the best'
- People telling me I was young
- Being told what I must do
- Being forced to eat
- Being forced to be sociable
- Not being able to buy a family ticket for outings
- Meeting new people
- Explaining my situation
- Financial, emotional, physical and spiritual worries
- Having no control over events
- Not knowing others' minds
- Receiving letters addressed to my late husband
- Not having extended family near
- Having to sell our family home
- Being in a 'couple society'
- Feeling I didn't fit in anymore
- Being both mother and father to the children
- Watching my peers getting on with their lives while feeling that I hadn't got one
- Paying bills and balancing books
- Insensitive remarks
- Not being able to be in two places at once
- Having too much to do in keeping us alive and well
- Not having language to adequately describe the depth of sadness and pain that my husband's suicide brought
- The prolonged intense grieving process
- My relationship with my husband being held up for public scrutiny

VULNERABILITY: I experienced feelings of great vulnerability. I was open, raw, weak and sensitive inside. My world was a

place to be in, and in order to survive I put up barriers to
otect myself from even more hurt and pain. Very, very slowly
these barriers had to come down and they did so when I
became more confident and at ease with both myself and my
surroundings.

CHAPTER FOUR

The Children's Grief

THE DEATH OF THEIR FATHER left the children puzzled and sad at the loss. The adult concept of death was far beyond the understanding of their young minds, and they felt that in some way they had caused their father to go away. Great hurt surrounded their father's death, and even though the smaller children were easily distracted, they still kept coming back to the unresolved mystery of death. The children's ages ranged from ten years down to two years when their father died, and this made a difference in their memories, guilt and fears and their overall effects and reactions.

The eldest child was devastated on hearing the news. She looked shocked and pale and confused as to what was expected of her. Her relationship with her father had left a lot to be desired as she was aware of what was going on around her. In her innocent confusion she felt guilty for not wanting to be in his company and thought that if she had acted differently he would not have killed himself. This child needed to be told over and over again that it was not her fault and that no one was to blame as it was her father's decision to die. This child had witnessed so much in her short life that my heart went out to her. She was bright and articulate and was able to voice her fears; this was beneficial as it meant she didn't bottle up too many fears and concerns. My daughter knew that I was available to her at any time and she returned hug for hug. She greeted well-wishers and accepted their condolences with a quiet dignity that was far beyond her tender years. In order to keep herself busy and to be helpful she handed out tea and sandwiches and generally helped out in the kitchen.

During the early days of bereavement I was very aware of how she became a 'stand-in' mother to the younger ones when I wasn't free to attend to them. She also saw that the animals were fed and cared for and undertook such tasks without complaint. This child became my right-hand woman and showed strength of character and an unspoken understanding that made me feel very humbled.

Visits from close school friends had a tremendously positive effect on this eldest child. They provided a comfort and a reassurance that such friendships were constant and would continue. In this respect, nothing had changed. One particular friend whose father had died some years previously was particularly helpful in letting my daughter see that life as she knew it wouldn't be completely changed and that it was possible to overcome her loss. Such a friend also demonstrated that my daughter wasn't the only one to lose a parent. These friends also helped in the kitchen and took it upon themselves to remain at my daughter's side even when she just wanted to sit on her bed and cry. These girls acted like guardian angels for my daughter and I was very glad for them to do so. Realising that these girls were still at primary school and were able to demonstrate such compassion and comradeship was truly amazing.

The second child was only seven years and he reacted differently from the eldest. He became very quiet and withdrawn and sat on the stairs silently, generally unobserved, as he watched and listened to all that was going on around him. This concerned me a little as I had to be with well-wishers and couldn't spend as much time with him as I wanted. I was concerned that he was hearing conversations discussing his father's suicide, and cautioned adults that there were young ears listening. This little boy passively watched my every move and firmly understood the implications of his father's death. When I saw his pale, sad face my heart ached and I felt as if it would explode in my chest. This little boy seemed so lost and bewildered. I hugged him and reassured him that all would be well and that we'd all stay together. I told him that I'd love and care for him.

The next child was four years old and his reactions were a mixture of his elder siblings. He tried to be as helpful as possible and busied himself with minor tasks. In this respect he was more mobile and active than his brother. This child was very protective of me and would tell me to come and sit down beside him and often would just come up and give me a kiss and a hug. He played constantly with a toy helicopter while dangling his legs over a kitchen stool. This boy understood that his father wouldn't be coming back. His main concerns were that we wouldn't move back to our former home, as he liked his new one better, and that I wouldn't die and leave him as well. He also watched and listened to the well-wishers and was able to repeat conversations and ask me what certain words meant.

The youngest, being only two years, was confused as to what exactly was going on. She became very clingy and wouldn't let me out of her sight. She stuck to me like superglue and wouldn't part with either her soother or her comfort blanket. When people spoke to her she'd hide her head in my shoulder and refuse to acknowledge them, yet at other times she had asked well-wishers if they knew that her daddy was dead and up in heaven. This question really put some people on the spot and they'd struggle in their embarrassment at responding. I recall one occasion when she pulled and tugged at a man's overcoat until he gave her his attention, 'excuse me, excuse me', she repeated, 'why did my daddy die?'

It was hard for me to talk and greet callers with this child clinging on to me. When she had her afternoon nap it left me free to accept hugs and kisses from others and to have my four-year-old son sit on my knee for a while.

Dressing the children for their father's funeral was very trying for me as the boys reacted badly to wearing shirt and ties, and the youngest absolutely refused to wear anything except her multicoloured tights and her pink dress. I had explained as clearly as possible what was entailed in a funeral service and burial. Each child held a flower to place on their father's coffin. Seeing the coffin was very difficult for the eldest, she broke down and sobbed uncontrollably. The boys didn't show the same reaction and just stood together in silence, while the youngest was oblivious to most of the proceedings. She held her comfort blanket close to her face. The children were pleased to see the familiar faces of their teachers and school friends as they scanned the faces in the crowds. Once the service had been completed the children were only too glad to return home as they were tired, stressed, cold and hungry.

In the days following their father's funeral, the two younger children played at burying a teddy bear. I watched as they ceremoniously carried a large teddy bear, one at its head and the other at its feet. Slowly they walked the length of the hallway and back again before placing it in a box on the carpet. They took it in turns to say prayers over the teddy before repeating the whole process over again. Watching such scenes was hard for me, but I knew that this play was their way of coming to terms with all they had witnessed.

Now that the house was back into some form of routine
and callers were less frequent, I was available to speak to each
child in turn. Night-times seemed to bring the children's
concerns more to the fore. The eldest questioned me about
why her father had to die and leave us all, why he wouldn't
accept help and why God didn't do something to prevent the
tragedy. She was obsessed with one main concern and that was
who would bury her if she was the last person alive on earth.
My answers were as truthful and simplistic as I could make
them. The oldest boy had many profound questions that
touched me greatly. He wanted to know why we were alive on
earth if we had to die anyway, he asked why people hadn't
helped when I'd asked them, and he wanted to know why his
father's relatives blamed me for the death. He also was
concerned about where his father's soul was and if would be
punished for his suicide.

The boy of four wanted to know what it was like to die and
wondered if he'd die too. He wanted reassurances that he
would be loved and cared for and that he wouldn't have to go
anywhere that he didn't want to go and that included going
back to our previous family home. He loved the bungalow that
was now our home. He was also concerned with what would
happen to his father's body in the grave and if it would stay
there or be lifted up to heaven.

The youngest child had no questions whatsoever. As long as
she had her soother, her comfort blanket, her kitten and her
video tapes of *Supergirl* and *The Sound of Music* she was content
enough.

Once the elder children returned to school they settled
down very quickly indeed, which left the youngest at home
with me. We spent our time together in peace and harmony
with her colouring in and drawing pictures and me doing
housework. Some of her drawings were made using only a

black crayon and depicted scenes of funerals and graves with people wiping tears from their eyes. On one occasion, when I suggested that she draw a picture of her family for putting up on the wall, she just sat and looked at a blank white page. When I asked her why she wasn't drawing she stood up and kicked her chair crying that she didn't have a family anymore. I learnt a great deal from her drawings about what was going on in her mind and was able then to talk with her and alleviate her confusion and fears.

The children's primary school was very well prepared for their return. The headmaster greeted them in assembly and said a special prayer in remembrance of their late father. Teachers were sensitive in their dealings with the children and watched for bereavement bullying. On Father's Day, the children were given tasks to busy themselves with when the rest of their class friends made Father's Day cards.

I tried to give each individual child time alone with me and on one such occasion I took my four year old son for a special treat. He had a certain amount of money to spend and was encouraged to choose something that he really wanted from a large toy store. After taking a long time to choose, he decided upon a kite. Proudly he approached the counter with his purchase and watched as it was wrapped for him. The shopkeeper told him that he had chosen wisely and that his daddy would help him assemble it when he got home. My little son looked at me as if to say 'will I or won't I say anything?' I smiled down at him and gave him a nod allowing him to make his own decision. He said nothing. Outside of the shop I asked why he hadn't explained to the man that his daddy was dead and his words touched me greatly. This little four year old said, 'I didn't tell the man because I didn't want him to be sad.'

Another incident involving my eldest boy showed me exactly how he was feeling. He was sitting in the back of a friend's car as the boy's father drove them to a football match. Suddenly a car pulled out in front of them, which forced this man to break suddenly and declare 'That was close. We nearly ended up in heaven with the angels,' to which my son replied, 'then I'm glad we didn't, as some people have told me that my father is up in heaven with the angels and I don't want to be where he is.' Such a comment from my son shocked this man. To this present day he and his wife are a source of great friendship for us all.

While driving past our previous family home one evening, after it had been sold, the youngest child noticed a light on and cried out, 'Mummy, daddy's back'. Her comment hit hard as I tried to explain the concept of death to her all over again. Such incidents served to demonstrate how each child's understanding and perceptions of their father's death differed, and how I had to listen carefully to what was being said in order to best help them.

As the children grew and developed they needed a 'top up' chat from me in order to have all concerns out in the open. As their awareness grew so did their need for deeper explanations. Their school coursework required discussions on abortion, euthanasia and suicide, so they had been well prepared in advance and didn't find it too difficult a task. The role of drama now plays an important part in schools where pupils act out difficulties and find solutions for their problems. While this is a good exercise, great sensitivity is called for when dealing with children who have experienced a loss by suicide.

It has now been sixteen years since their father's death and all my children are now young adults. Some have lost close friends to suicide and faced more loss in their lives. These tragic acts also opened up old wounds for them, which had to be dealt with and addressed. They now had adult reasoning and logic as well as a spiritual awareness to help them through these difficult times.

Each offspring is unique with individual personalities. They are well adjusted physically, emotionally and spiritually. They are making their own way in the wider world and I like to think that I have done a good job in rearing them single handedly. They are open, loving and ready to offer a healing and helping hand to those who need it. We are all still a united group and I feel very proud of them. My eldest daughter is now just a few years away from being the age I was when their father died. She is in awe of this fact and asks how I coped. Recently she gave me a great compliment by saying that if she has children she'd rear them in exactly the same way that I had reared her. She said that she had wanted for nothing and felt no different in not having a father's presence as I had always been there for the special events in her life, and more importantly, I had been there for her when she returned home from school.

The eldest boy is now very much his own person and is wise beyond his years; the youngest boy is a very sociable and sensitive being and still looks out for me. Often it seems as if the roles are reversing and he's becoming the parent to me. The youngest child is now eighteen years and is preparing to fly the nest with the rest of her school year. I feel she suffered the most from never having known a father figure and as a result can feel hard done by at times.

The children's reactions throughout their grieving included:

- Feeling shocked
- Feeling confused
- Feeling low in spirits and depressed
- Being fearful
- Feeling lonely
- Feeling relief
- Having mixed and difficult emotions
- Feeling guilt and blame

- Feeling unlovable
- Angry
- Suicidal fantasies

While the children firstly longed for things to be as they were, for normality, they seemed to adjust to a life without their father. It was best for me not to assume that I knew what they were feeling, but rather to ask and then accept what they told me. Each child experienced grief in his or her own way and I found the following guidelines to be helpful in managing their grief:

- Being as honest as possible with them
- Repeating over and over facts and information suitable for the child's level of understanding
- Encouraging the expression of their grief in safety
- Clearing up fantasies and misconceptions with honesty and simplicity
- Encouraging relaxation in the children by firstly relaxing myself, as children learn from observation
- Giving leisure time for fun and laughter to take the focus away from death
- Never telling them more than they wanted to know, or even needed to know
- Giving short and truthful explanations
- Reassuring them that they would be loved and cared for
- Being available physically and emotionally at all times
- Using clear and uncomplicated words
- Allowing the children's voices to be heard and giving them a minor part in the funeral and burial services
- Not telling the children that they were brave as this only implies that it was wrong for them to be upset
- People who know the children well were best to guide and make allowances for them

- It was best not to leave the children to pick up on tense atmospheres as they often imagined something far worse than the reality
- Being warm, loving and open and never rejecting

It wasn't easy being both mother and father, but it was a privilege to see innocent children through a tough and a traumatic grief reaction. Children have wonderful adaptive abilities and can overcome even the most punitive of circumstances, provided that they are given a secure base filled with consistent and constant love and protection.

CHAPTER FIVE

Remembrances of a First Christmas

CHRISTMAS IS A TIME that awakens the strongest and most heart-felt associations. This festive season, which commerates the religion of peace and love, has rightly been made the season for the gathering together of family. For those who are experiencing a first Christmas without a loved one present it can be a daunting time that only serves to remind them of adversity, misfortune and loss.

For me the first Christmas loomed ominously and I feared it would pass like a slow train in the darkness, roaring and vanishing while taking part of me with it and leaving behind even more suffering, pain, regret and sorrow. It demanded every ounce of my mental, physical and emotional energy.

During this time of crowded pleasures and close neighbourliness, when friendly sympathies are more aroused, many good tidings were lost on ears and eyes that had been closed by grief. Through our dependence upon one another for enjoyment, love, generosity and devotion, the children and myself bonded together closely. We shared tears, food, smiles, talk, love and of course, our loss.

My husband and the children's father had vanished out of sight and had shrunk away. The children's vision of their late father was a happy picture of him in heaven attending a party filled with angels of joy and having fun. I recall clearly an episode when the youngest child took my hand and led me into a bedroom where a friend's new baby slept undisturbed and, as I thought, unnoticed by my daughter. My little girl pointed to the carrycot that was placed upon the bed, and kneeling down whispered 'baby Jesus has come and Christmas is here'. Watching my child's simplicity and spontaneity of devotion as she admired and held the baby's hand moved me greatly. At that moment it seemed as if a light had come on and banished the darkness and gloom around me. This touching innocence served to remind me of where I was and of my responsibilities.

The decorations were up and every room in the house lit up like a star. The Christmas tree had pride of place in the hallway, with presents placed beneath. The children and myself were inundated with gifts and tokens of Christmas. My eldest son celebrated his birthday near to Christmas day and we held a small party for his close friends. Balloons and poppers were very much in vogue and it was good to see the children enjoying themselves and to hear laughter ringing out again.

Many people remembered us that first Christmas and many cars were parked outside our bungalow, so much so that one child commented that the neighbours would think that someone else had died in our house!

In the week leading up to Christmas, the bungalow was broken into as we slept soundly, and my handbag with the remainder of our money was stolen. This incident only served to reinforce my sense of vulnerability and lack of control over life. At least, I reasoned, we weren't harmed, and the Christmas presents beneath the tree hadn't been touched. This incident required the police to visit the home and it reminded me of their visit on my husband's death. They were kindness itself and searched a nearby field where my handbag was found, minus the money, but everything of sentimental value for me remained. When my eldest son turned to me as the police left he said, 'God what's going to happen next?' I couldn't answer him as I'd started to laugh at the irony of it all and soon all the other children had joined in and we laughed until the tears ran down our cheeks.

The children wanted to send friends Christmas cards and I thought 'why not?', after all it was a special time, and even though some relatives told us that it was not the 'done thing' in the first Christmas following a death, we sent out cards and good wishes to everyone we wanted to and experienced great pleasure in doing so. When the postman arrived with cards and parcels the children fought over who should be allowed to open them, but once a shared agreement was made everyone was happy.

Christmas Eve was a magical one. We attended an evening service in church and joined the congregation in singing hymns and entered into the spirit of kinship and anticipation of what was to come the following day. The youngest child spent this service in front of the crib of the baby Jesus, never touching but always looking. We had to drag her away when the service was over. Her crib at home didn't hold the same appeal for her. I found the singing of the hymns and the organ music to be very emotive, and gazing as the light from flickering candles illuminated the stain glass windows, my senses became flooded with the beauty of it all and I had to fight to keep my emotions in check.

Back at home, when the younger children were in bed and dreaming of Santa's gifts, close friends called and brought with them a model of a Barbie House that was to be Santa's present for my little daughter. We opened up the box and looked at the instructions – they may as well have been written in a foreign language for all the sense they made! My friend's husband confidently told us to leave it to him; he'd have no difficulty assembling it. Nor did he. He took the unassembled Barbie House home with him and put it together in next to no time. However, when it came to delivering the completed house back to our bungalow he found that he couldn't get it into his car. At two o'clock on Christmas morning he had to borrow a friend's trailer in order to deliver Santa's present before the youngest one would waken. This incident was hilarious and certainly helped to lighten our moods.

The Christmas Day that I had been dreading turned out to be a very peaceful and a contented one, despite remembering that a family member was missing. The meal was delicious, even though I wouldn't eat or swallow much of it. Crackers were pulled and jokes told, paper hats were worn and we all became very silly indeed. When friends and neighbours visited with good wishes we all joined in listening while the children played Christmas hymns on their violins and piano.

Presents took ages to open as there were so many gifts of generosity and the look of delight in the children's faces raised a smile on my own. Christmas evening was spent quietly calming down from the days' events by watching *The Sound of Music* and *It's A Wonderful Life*. We want to bed tired but happy and I sent up a prayer of thanks for a Christmas Day that would remain with me forever. Christmas Day was worthy of being dedicated and observed not only in remembrance of the blessed nativity of Jesus, but also in the remembrance of our deceased loved one.

CHAPTER SIX

Recovery Signs

A S TIME PASSED healing really did take place, and no matter how much despair and anguish were experienced it was possible to go beyond grief and loss and recognise life in a new and a more meaningful way. It required honesty, openness and a flexibility to change. It may have taken a long time before we felt in any way normal again and experienced joy and happiness, but in time it was possible to erase painful memories, overcome difficulties and to even review our relationship with significant others.

Nothing now will ever seem shameful, embarrassing or humiliating again. In becoming less passive and doing things for ourselves we shifted from being negative to becoming more positive; we no longer felt incomplete.

Following the suicide of my husband there was an invitation for growth to illuminate the darkness and heal our broken hearts. Life is sacred, so it was important to learn to enjoy every moment and to look forward to the future in a more positive manner – wiser, more aware and far more compassionate and understanding. As survivors of a loved one's tragic suicide we developed and matured, no longer feeling so tense, anxious, guilty, angry, depressed and unsafe in a huge hostile world. We moved on to leave behind the role of helpless and hopeless victims and transformed our lives with vitality and energy, finding joy even in the simplest of things. We learnt to be thankful for all the blessings in our lives, and that included the loved one who was lost to us.

The bereavement process unfolded itself at its natural pace and couldn't be hurried. At six months I felt grief acutely and I longed to be free from all the physical, emotional and spiritual symptompathology that engulfed and overwhelmed me. I wanted to live life to the full and I didn't want to feel so hard done by or that there was no justice in this life. My experience of hell was being blocked from God by my own feelings of anger towards Him. I faced many difficult choices involving divided loyalties and intense needs.

Firstly, I had to recognise the fact that it was I who was experiencing grief and it was I who had to somehow find a way through it. This didn't mean that I would be churlish enough not to accept help and guidance from close friends and advisers. I made my decision to remain at home in order to be a constant and a secure presence for the children. In not working I was always available when the children were sick or were on school holidays. It meant that I could be present for school plays, sports days and parent-teacher meetings. Not having to rush out to work or to be at a certain place for a certain time ensured that I would have some quiet and quality time for myself, which I found very necessary indeed. Once the children were at their respective schools I could return home and quickly make beds, tidy up, prepare an evening meal and either go for a long walk along a nearby beach or read an uplifting book, watch a film with a positive ending, listen to spiritual music or receive visitors. I could also see friends for lunch and have a gossip, but most importantly I could visit my clergyman friend and receive a necessary fix of spiritual uplifting and renewal.

There were times when I'd feel drained with very little energy reserves to draw from, yet somehow I managed to keep going and do all that was required of me. When sitting through concerts, plays or family gatherings, I'd often long just to get up and leave. I'd feel stifled, overwhelmed and panicky. My concentration was very poor and trying to focus my attention on what was being said was difficult if not downright impossible. My senses were heightened, and when lights became too bright and the noise level too high I'd often find myself in precarious and unacceptable environments. I forced myself to go out socially, but only if I could leave when I wanted to, though making an acceptable excuse. I learnt to always drive to gatherings and in so doing became independent and in control of when I went home.

My defences were erected and surrounded me like a suit of armour. I was not prepared to let anyone close enough to either hurt me or see me so vulnerable. In a way the unconscious messages that I gave out were 'keep away' and 'I'm in control'. Only a few people knew the soft me beneath the surface and this was fine by me. My body language was tense and rigid and it was only in my own home that I could fully relax.

Driving long distances became a problem for me, mainly because I was feeling very tired all of the time, but also because I lacked concentration. I was definitely not safe on the roads and only by God's grace did I avoid accidents. I hated being away from home and all the security it presented, so holidays were not totally relaxing for me. They were great for the children, but I found them to be a bit of an ordeal. They seemed to emphasise the fact that I was now a single parent and alone with four little lives to protect and care for.

Everywhere I looked it seemed as if it was a coupled society and I didn't really fit into any group. I was single now, but not free because of the children, and I was no longer part of a couple. This fact helped to shake any sense of belonging and I felt somehow punished and ostracised as a result. My self-esteem was at rock bottom and my self-image became very shaky.

I was encouraged to have my hair cut and to 'smarten myself up'. I was assured that this would brighten me up and make me feel better. I did so and attended a neighbour's party where one female guest came up to me and called me 'the merry widow'. If she only knew how I was feeling inside. I was only thirty years old and felt that my life was over. My pride wouldn't allow me the satisfaction of retaliating, but those words hurt me deeply and had the effect of my becoming even more cut off from others whom I imagined were also watching and observing me. I learnt not to engage in conversations with male guests in case I'd upset their partners and by so doing was described as being 'anti-male'. One man told me that my problem was that I didn't need anyone in my life, that I was too independent and self-sufficient for my own good! So much for me trying not to give out the wrong signals. It never ceased to amaze me that total strangers felt the need to make such personal comments and remarks directly to me.

Sitting through religious ceremonies was also difficult, as I found them to be too long and the words spoken held little meaning for me. I made the effort to attend such services for the children's sakes as they attended schools where the continuation of religious instruction was essential. At church I met people who greeted me and always asked how I was. These people spoke gently to the children and always had a kind word for them. A difficulty for me was the fact that I would see my in-laws at certain church services and they only reinforced the attribution of blame in me. I often felt it was unchristian and cruel, if not unjust, but I learnt to rise above it and let go of all the negative feelings directed my way. The best times in church for me were the occasions when there were few people present and I could light a candle and quietly meditate until I felt the need to leave. Such serene times helped to recentre myself and gave me a place to go where I could be private for a time.

While driving along one day, the song *Whispering Hope* came on the radio and this song made me smile. It had been my 'party piece' and my song for solo performances at *feiseanna*. I sang along with the singer, but somehow the words now held more meaning for me and their message penetrated my brain and soul. Tears flowed as I was reminded not to falter in my hope as all would be well. How poignant that after all the years since my school days, 'my song' would pop up at the exact moment that became so necessary, helpful and special for me.

After the inquest was held and monies were released I decided to turn our little bungalow into a home by decorating it and planting a garden. A landscape gardener was recommended to me and I willingly gave him an advance of fifty pounds to buy the plants and seeds needed. I waited and waited for this gardener's return and I'm still waiting some sixteen years later. This incident served as my first lesson in money management and awareness, it also had the effect of shaking my ability for trusting even further. I became far more wary and felt even more vulnerable in transactions.

With the bungalow decorated and the garden finally planted I felt a change in my outlook. It was as if with every freshened up room and tidied cupboard the compartments in my brain became less cluttered and brighter. My energy levels rose and for the first time in ages I felt a renewal of spirits. In creating a home for the children, animals and myself, I created a little piece of heaven here on earth – or so it seemed to me! It was a home where the door was always open for visitors, the children's friends and, as it turned out, for any stray animal that the children found.

The change in me was recognised by those who knew me best. They could see that I no longer had a haunted look on my face, that my colour was better and that the dark circles beneath my eyes were gone.

On a point of principle I decided that enough was enough. In the future I was going to assert myself and gain more power over happenings in my life. I stood up straighter and looked people in the eye. I no longer cared about the good opinions of others. I knew what I'd experienced and lived through and never again would I let anyone speak down to me. I reasoned that I didn't deserve such treatment and I would no longer tolerate it. I also decided that if I didn't want to do something then I just wasn't going to do it no matter how pressurised I felt. I now became a force to be reckoned with as I stood up for myself and the children. I was like a lioness with her cubs.

The sleeping rebel inside of me had awakened and others saw it just by looking at the sparkle in my eyes. I no longer felt so vulnerable and exposed and came to the conclusion that no individual had or has the right to control another. I became like a bird after being trapped in a nest and who now was ready to fly. I had to overcome many childhood conditionings and family expectations in order to become 'just me'. Instead of gradually losing myself I was now ready to find out the 'real me', the 'whole me' and exactly what I was capable of becoming. I wouldn't conform to anyone or anything that didn't suit me. At times I longed for someone to look after me in tender, loving concern, but I decided that while I waited for such a person I would give all of this to myself – and I'd never let me down.

I made a list of all that was positive in my life, such as children, friends, family, a home, a car, which provided me with tremendous freedom and independence, my relatively good physical and mental health, and enough money to keep everything going if I balanced the books.

There were, of course, still limitations on my life, but I now accepted them by reasoning and saying, 'so what?' to myself. I knew I was in a stronger position where I could permit myself to ask for help if it was needed. I was not superwoman even if, at times, I was expected to be! I learnt to say no without causing offense and my self-esteem and self-worth rose sharply. I also decided that as a child of God I deserved to be treated with respect for doing a difficult job under difficult conditions and circumstances.

The children noticed that I didn't yawn or sigh as much and that I was more physically active and outward-looking, more relaxed, less tense and better able to find solutions for problems without taxing their patience too much. My mind became more alert and focused and I shifted my negative thoughts for more positive ones.

I knew now that I could survive and that the pain I'd experienced wouldn't kill me. I was well prepared for rearing four children single-handedly as I'd been doing so since they were born. The only difference now was that I didn't have the perceived security of a husband, a protector and a provider.

With my renewed awareness and sharpness of insight, I noticed a big change in all four children. It seemed that the more I healed and grew in confidence the more they did too. We all broke the chains that bound us to a situation that was no longer. The eldest girl moved with ease from her primary school to her secondary one. She matured and developed as if overnight. This girl became very lively, loving and sociable. She had a good balance between academic studies and recreation. Boys became a feature and she became less self-conscious and more than equal at standing up for her rights while debating a point of issue. She blossomed like a flower and I never had to ask her news, as she was always only too ready to share it with me.

In many ways the changes in her were awesome. She became a prefect and walked with a confident air. When the father of one of her friends died she was able to comfort this girl and give her hope for the future. At times she would speak of her late father and keep photographs and memorabilia in her room. She was proud that her father had reached the top of his profession at a young age and had been held in high esteem by many. This didn't mean that she had forgotten the not so good points to his character, but rather that she was able to concentrate on the positive rather than dwelling on the negative. At her secondary school she came across other girls from single-parent families so she didn't feel so different or unusual. This girl places a high value on herself and has a very kind and a tender heart. I am proud of her and of her many achievements in overcoming tragedy at such a tender and sensitive age. If there remains any residue of the difficulties encountered then, I knew she would be brave enough to take a step towards someone who would be able to talk through issues with her.

The eldest boy showed signs of recovery when he began to look healthier, less stressed and stopped watching out for my return if I was out of the house for any length of time. The dark circles left his eyes and he became more relaxed, laid back and at ease. He had a fantastic 'father figure stand-in' in the shape of a school friend's father. This man was an angel in disguise. There wasn't a week went by when football or miniature golf didn't feature. This boy became very sports-orientated and an outdoors person. He began to tell jokes and laugh heartily again. He was very loving, affectionate and caring towards me and if I were alright then he was too. He became a member of a Scouts group and enjoyed attaining goals and being rewarded with badges. He liked nothing better than caravanning, fishing, freezing rabbits with a torch in the dark and mountain climbing. He healed in so many ways, becoming confident enough to speak his mind openly.

If he saw or heard of an injustice, he confronted it and often got into trouble for speaking plainly, but I was proud that he felt able to be so vocal. When he passed to secondary school he became very much his own person and was made a prefect. If I asked him his news I was met by a wall of silence so I learnt not to ask and just to wait patiently until, sooner or later, he'd give me bits and pieces of relevant information.

At school this boy was quiet and mixed well and only spoke up directly when asked a question. His form teacher informed me that he'd have a great career in the diplomatic corps, as he'd give nothing away! He was polite, well mannered and not easily led. Being the eldest son he took it upon himself to lock up the house at nighttimes. In his final year of school he lost three friends by natural causes. His mature approach at visiting the bereaved homes and attending the funerals gave me cause for pride and I felt that I had done a good job in rearing this young man.

The third boy needed his confidence built up so whenever he undertook a task and completed it I'd praise him. He was very sensitive to criticism and could be tearful and needing reassurances when something or someone upset him. At school he settled in well and soon made friends. As the days and weeks passed he coped better with the changes and soon found his own level. This boy would always pop in to check that I was still at home when he was playing outside. I knew that he feared me dying and leaving him alone so I assured him that I had no intention of going anywhere.

As he became less fearful and more secure in himself this boy grew and developed into a very caring and mature individual. He was always ready to help anyone who needed it and was so patient and gentle that his goodness shone out of his face. This boy also became very sport-orientated and played football and golf. He became physically very broad and tall at an early age and would pass for a much older boy. This had the negative effect that he was expected to behave older than he was.

When he entered the bigger school he took a little longer than his brother to settle in, but grew into a very assured and reliable young man. He also became a prefect and enjoyed his school years greatly. When a close friend took his own life unexpectedly it reawakened and opened up old wounds for my son. We talked concerns over and his class had counselling with the school counsellor, so all worries were, hopefully, dealt with. He paid a visit to the bereaved household and paid tribute to his friend at the funeral. This demonstrated a strength of character and I couldn't help but feel very proud of him.

The youngest child's progression in overcoming grief was in many ways easier for me to recognise. Her drawings became less and less black and brighter and more colourful. Rainbows and sandy beaches, sandcastles, white clouds in a blue sky and happy smiling people became features. She became less clingy and needed her soothers and comfort blanket less and less until one day she threw her soother into the bin. Her questions about her daddy faded and she became more confident and outgoing while playing with friends outdoors. Her need to come into my bed at night also lessened until finally she slept soundly and undisturbed in her own bedroom. As time progressed she made new friends at nursery school and her social world widened.

Days turned into weeks and months into years. Her move to primary school was easier for her as her two elder brothers were already there. The school was only a short distance from our home and soon I could wave all three goodbye in the morning as they walked to school – with our beloved cat following behind.

Primary school was a happy place for her as she grew and developed in confidence, knowledge and self-assurance. I believe that she was spoilt a little by everyone as she was the youngest in the family and looked angelic with blond hair and blue eyes. The boys and her older sister often complained that she 'got off with murder' and that this state of affairs was unjust. I did try to balance everything out, but it proved to be difficult as she never pushed or fought to get her way, her tongue did all the lashing for her.

When she moved to secondary school she followed in her big sister's footsteps and hated being compared to her. She prized her individuality and was a non-conformist at heart. When she became a prefect she had to enforce rules that inwardly made little sense to her. This girl does feel the loss of a father in her life and has no memories to draw upon. She had to make do with photographs and stories of 'when she was a baby'. I believe she feels the injustice of her father's suicide acutely at times and my hope is that she will find a level of acceptance and understanding as she fully matures.

I hope my efforts and dedication in rearing all four children will pay dividends in their lives and that any long term effects of such a traumatic experience in their tender years will have a minimal effect on their adult lives.

Chapter Seven

Finding My Step

FOLLOWING MY HUSBAND'S suicide, well-meaning people often asked if I had any 'sense' of my late husband's presence around the children and myself. I honestly replied that I didn't. During those dark days I was too bewildered and overwhelmed to 'sense' anything and I wasn't even sure if I wanted to have any 'sense' of my late husband at all. I remembered all too clearly the frustrations, moodiness and criticisms directed at me and how all of my suggestions and offers of help would be turned aside and dismissed with sarcasms and insults.

I was angry and resentful at my late husband for daring to 'opt out' and leave myself and the children behind to clear up a mess that was not of our doing. This was so typical of my husband's behaviour – he'd often create a scene causing great upset and disharmony before walking away and leaving the calming of the children and the rectifying of wrong doings to me. The only difference on this occasion was that my husband would not be coming back – this time his walking out was permanent. He had crossed the path of no return.

I functioned as I normally did, by developing the necessary adaptive reflexes that hid my innermost concerns and fears. My face used to be an open book as far as feelings were concerned, but I soon mastered the art of concealment.

My professional life had previously afforded opportunities for speaking with people who shared their near-death experiences with me. Their accounts of unconditional love in an all embracing, welcoming light moved me greatly and I hoped that my late husband had experienced a similar greeting. I began reading spiritual literature and books that encompassed all of life and the more I learnt the more I longed to know. It was as if I had developed an overwhelming need to understand this great mystery of life and the reasons behind the long road that had brought me to this moment in life.

It has been said that when the pupil is ready the teacher will appear and this is exactly what I experienced. It seemed that no sooner had I thought of a question than an answer was given to me either directly or indirectly. The more knowledge I gained the more I felt it to be true, as if part of me had this knowledge already. To begin with I felt the need to debate the exchange of information with others and to share my knowledge and learnings in safe, familiar surroundings where I wouldn't be discredited or criticised. However, as time progressed I was made aware of the need for caution in becoming over enthusiastic in sharing too much information with those who were not yet ready to handle it. I learnt that ideas have to evolve gradually and at a pace that suits the individual. I began to shift the focus from outside of myself to within. Sitting quietly in prayer and meditation I developed and established a private dialogue with God while continually asking for answers to questions that concerned me.

Listening to relaxing background music enabled me to repress many of the concerns of traumatic grief, while walks along the sea shores provided respite from the struggles and routines of daily life. The full realisation came to me that God cannot be confirmed in any shape or form but rather is to be found everywhere, in us and in nature. The closer I moved towards Him the closer He moved towards me and I recalled clearly the promises that He made to us:

- Take one step towards me and I'll take ten towards you
- Ask and it shall be given
- Shed one tear and I will wipe a hundred from your eyes

Healing and forgiving came very slowly and gradually. Bringing up four children alone is a very tough and a demanding job even if it is an incredibly rewarding one. While watching the children grow, develop and reach their milestones, I often thought about their late father and wondered if he ever felt sorrow at the pain and hurt he had left behind. I wondered if he somehow saw the children on the special days of their lives when a father would feature strongly. Such days were always tinged with sadness for us all.

During one of my quiet times with God I spoke from the heart and asked for a sign or a message that my late husband's soul was at peace. Over the years I had learnt to be relaxed in knowing that my prayers or requests would, somehow, be answered, but even now I smile at just how this information was given to me – as a saying goes: 'God moves and walks in mysterious ways'. A few days after making this request my elder daughter phoned me from abroad where she was on holiday with friends. Sounding her usual cheerful and excited self she asked me to sit down as she had some marvellous news for me. Being in a holiday mood the girls had decided to have their fortunes told for a 'bit of craic'. Taking it all with a pinch of salt my daughter was the first to have her reading.

The person doing the reading introduced herself by saying that she was a psychic, a medium and a clairvoyant. Smiling at my daughter she told her that the spirit of her late father wished to pass on a message of information that her mother had been seeking. The message given was that my late husband had been in turmoil for some time prior to his death and also during his passing but that he had been led into the light by a deceased parent. He was healed and at peace and sending loving healing light to us all. With great accuracy my daughter was given more detailed information concerning her brothers and younger sister and a brighter future was predicted for one and all.

My daughter had gone to have her fortune told for entertainment purposes only, but she was so excited by all that she had been told that she kept saying 'Can you believe this mum?' and 'Isn't this really weird?' While I sat quietly with the telephone receiver in my hand I sent up a prayer of thanks to God for giving me the information that I sought. I know some people have a certain caution and a somewhat fearful view of psychics, but I believe that all knowledge comes from God and that He uses many channels and people in helping others.

The message given to me was very uplifting and was exactly what I wished for my late husband – peace and healing in the light of God. It also demonstrated that when truth is desired it will be given. Such survival evidence greatly refreshed me mentally, physically and spiritually. It also renewed my confidence and brought me an inner peace and calm. The news also freed me from holding on to something and to someone who no longer needed me. It encouraged me to move on with my own life in the knowledge that we are only ans~~~~ ~~~~ our own actions and not for those of othe

Such a message was also marvellous ı the belief that our loved ones aren't lost t continue to live, be it in a different form. T eternal can never be extinguished, and promised will come about. We will be united with all our loved ones when the time is right. My personal life experiences have allowed me to step back and understand far more than could possibly be taught at colleges or universities.

Without a shadow of a doubt I believe that none of us are required to be superhuman. We have our own limitations and so are not capable of handling all of our problems alone. We need to surrender all troubles and anger to God with humility and reverence. In staying close to God we are able to avoid feelings of despair and futility towards life. God doesn't make mistakes and nothing happens without his consent so those who take their own lives are not judged harshly but are treated with gentle understanding and loving concern. They are taken into the light when the time is right and healed. We are on earth for a purpose with particular roles and lessons to learn and teach.

Through our intuitions, hunches and inner feelings we can recognise the synchronicity that guides our paths and we will meet those whom we are meant to meet. We have to look, ask, knock and venture from truth and answers. Through our unique experiences we will then be able to find the greater part of ourselves, that which seeks to act kindly by uplifting and helping others. By slowing down and making the time to demonstrate compassion we can give unconditional love and positive regard. Those of use who have learnt through suffering have a strong desire to reach out to those in pain. In having to create my own path through grief, I have been led to becoming the person that I've always meant to be. I don't have to be perfect and am free to express the highest truths that I know through radical, spontaneous self-expression. Many influences have surrounded me in my soul's development and in my spiritual awakening, but they do not ultimately define me. I can ow simply be myself without regard to the opinions of others have learnt to release my attachment to positive reviews. I

have a dream that the best is yet to be in
travelled an extraordinary path, I feel ready
evolutionary future filled with spiritual wo
being emotionally open and helpful to others
them to talk freely and openly about their fears and concerns,
rather than hiding them in the background of their lives.

Deep down inside of me I knew that I was born with a
mission and that my sense of meaning in life depended on my
fulfilling it. I knew that it somehow involved sustaining my
serenity in the face of life's onslaughts as well as facing my
wounds squarely and honestly while having an unshakable
sense of meaning in my life. I suppose one could describe it as
being a trans-personal purpose in life.

Throughout my quest for discovering exactly what my tasks
were in this life I discovered a deeper sense of my own
spirituality that helped me greatly as I worked through my
grief, and fitted together the massive jigsaw puzzle that was my
life to date. Firstly I had to dissolve the belief that I was
unworthy and that there was basically something wrong with
me. I had to accept the fact that I was indeed worthy and that
as a child of God I was part of his creation and not separate
from Him. I also had to reinforce the belief that I was lovable
and worthy of bringing the light of understanding to my life
experiences.

I was challenged to find the spiritual warrior within myself
and meditation enabled me to be brave and clear enough to
claim my own path and follow it. Society tries to seduce us into
prematurely accepting some role that doesn't have much to do
with individual nature or values. I needed to get my priorities
straight and be true to myself in order to overcome the forces
of peer pressure and the 'pull of the tribe'. I learnt to be true to
my own heart and to follow what was right for my own spirit.
I also needed a new vision, a new insight and the reshaping and

review of my philosophy or religion. This required delicate psychological, physical and emotional balancing.

One way in which my religious vision changed and intensified was in my relationship with Jesus. As a child, I learnt with sadness about Jesus; His life, His suffering and His death. It did not make any sense to me that He had to suffer for our sins and that His death on the cross somehow held meaning and hope for the whole of mankind. Now, after experiencing my own small suffering, I could identify more with the life and meaning of Jesus. I could identify with His longing to be heard, His frustrations, His aching for human company to watch with Him through a night of pain and anguish and how His love for innocent children made him a magnet for them. But mostly and mainly I finally understood why Jesus came to earth, and how His actions and death were for each and every one of us. To see ourselves as being separate from God and from each other is an illusion. We are all connected to one another and if someone performs an act of kindness it has a rebound affect upon us all at a very subtle level. Similarly, if someone performs an unkind act then it, too, has an effect on us all. This reasoning is now very much part of my vision of life's meaning and purpose, so if I can think loving thoughts, perform kind acts and create a harmonious environment then at some level I'm doing so for mankind as a whole. We are all spiritually of one body.

While I could not remember why I came to earth I knew that there were clues and coincidences along the way. I knew that I faced a profound spiritual challenge that involved steeling myself in the face of indecision and people-pleasing. It took me one step at a time and slow, steady, plodding before my mission became known to me.

Firstly, I needed energy for improving my surroundings and life situation. I needed a new beginning that involved altering

my view of the world and the shedding of many illusions. I
meditated daily with great enthusiasm and could feel the life
force within grow stronger as a result. I was surrounded by
peace and learnt to let go of anger, judgement, fear and self-
blame. My motivation for daily meditation was to gain
knowledge and truths by accessing the wisdom within. I learnt
to focus on listening for my inner voice or intuition in a calmer
and a peaceful manner. I also knew that I'd have to shift any
remaining doubts about material, financial and psychological
security and let my Higher source provide for us. The only real
control that we have is over ourselves. Practice makes perfect
and slowly I learnt to let go of all attempts to control while
continuing to work a little bit more on understanding myself
and my mission here on earth.

To begin with, I turned our new bungalow into a place of
colour, light and comfort. It became a home for all of us and for
our animals. The children were encouraged to bring friends to
visit and to stay. It became a home filled with laughter and fun.
Humour can be found even in the most difficult of times and I
will always treasure this time spent with the children. There is
no way to happiness – happiness *is* the way – so I learnt to be
appreciative of every moment that we had together. When I
took full responsibility for my life the bottomless pit of
helplessness became filled with power and love.

Everyone was welcome and I found great delight in having
friends over for meals and chats. I developed organisational
abilities that previously weren't apparent to me and while at
times I felt rebellious and had the need for freedom, I never
feared feelings of being out of control or veering off from my
given path. Being human is indeed tough at times, but watching
how animals live can be an example for how we should live our
lives. They show such devotion and unconditional love and face
hardships with a quiet dignity. They have their playtime and rest

time and appear contented with their experience of their world.

I loved digging in the garden, planting seeds and taking part in the beauty of nature while the children and animals played around me. I liked nothing better than to curl up with my cats while reading and listening to music and each day I sent up a little prayer of thanks for our little piece of heaven on earth. I reasoned that the children would carry this loving and secure place with them out into the wider world and even to the greater universe itself. Creating my special environment also included those around me and I ensured that significant others were of a positive disposition, which helped to lighten my situation so that it became less overwhelming. I found that negative people only exhausted me and I felt drained in their company. I learnt to walk away from people who treated me unkindly. With kindred people feeding my spirit I felt centred and at ease with myself. I became vibrant and enthused with life-force, so much so that I literally grew into my power. Communication, awareness and considerate words can do much healing and expand horizons and after sorrow comes great joy.

With my new strength and awareness, I looked back to see my path and recognised the synchronicity that had guided it. I no longer considered myself a victim focusing on what I'd been through, rather I knew that I was here on earth to experience life and I would accept it with integrity, without shame or guilt in a deep nurturing joy. I am worthy and I count. I am honourable in my vulnerability and I send out and radiate peace while seeing the world as a friendly place.

My mission as I perceived it was threefold, involving:

1.   The blowing a whistle on lies
2.   Countering evil and healing its effects
3.   Courage to speak out at the level of moral principle

And I like to think that I've carried out my tasks to the best of by ability.

Task One: Involved me standing alone and ignoring all threats and put-downs in order to bring my husband's behaviour and lies out into the open. It involved me being accused of lies and over-reacting to the situation behind our closed doors.

Task Two: Involved me undoing a lot of the harm imposed upon us by my late husband's behaviour. It also involved forgiving and letting go, and seeing the children and myself through our traumatic grief reactions. It saw me creating a piece of heaven here on earth and rearing children in a loving and secure environment while bringing the knowledge of a loving God into our lives. It saw the changing of all negatives into the positive, which had profound healing not only for us five, but also for mankind as a whole.

Task Three: I have always hated being the centre of attention, so my speaking and writing openly about my experience of bereavement by suicide requires a lot of courage in order to 'tell it as it is'. The reasons I do so are because in sharing my experiences the voices of all those who have lost a loved one to suicide are heard. Awareness of such pain and loss is heightened, as is the fact that with God's love and guidance it is possible to overcome and transcend grief and to live a life transformed by having shared time with someone special who now lives on at a different level. I am more open and comfortable with paranormal perceptions, including life reviews, and recognising predestined coincides. I know that while life is about survival it is also about spiritual evolution and the experience of joy as our natural state, i.e. when we die or pass over to Spirit we are shown our lives as we have lived them and we judge ourselves as to how much we feel we've achieved or not as the case may be.

It was spiritually very important for me to be heard after so much thinking, experiencing, learning and wondering. I needed to communicate and gather ideas while caring about the hurts that other humans suffer. Instinctively I try to sooth hurts and 'home in' on sources of pain.

I see my relationship with my husband as being an assignment, a vast plan for enlightenment and for greater awareness and expansion in order to find the greater part of myself, via looking, asking, experiencing and searching for what is sacred. I believe that my late husband learnt about love in his lifetime and that, despite his choice of passing, he carried that love on with him and fully experienced it when he was healed in the light. Now I can handle difficulties more easily and see them as being part of a larger story. I've learnt what really counts and no longer freeze in despair, rather I am able to just kick back and enjoy myself in a spirit of playfulness and creativity.

I believe that we are evolving through humanity's ultimate destiny – spiritualisation of our bodies and of all human culture on earth. We are all spiritual beings having a human experience. We are in this world, but not of it, and our true identity lies with God.

Now is the time for me to change and find a different path that somehow involves a role in which I address the hurts in the lives of others, and to let my mission coalesce before my eyes. My difficult pathway has given me strength of character and a compassion for feeling another's suffering, while knowing, without a doubt, that a Higher power will see us all through in an appropriate way. It involves acknowledgment and facing up to our predicaments or our situations while being able to rise above them and let them go. It is only God who knows what's best in the soul's journey, passage or evolution.

We should listen to our hearts while being true to our souls. The knowledge that we can handle anything is, to me, true security. What stopped me crying was my oneness with God and the knowledge that I didn't have to remain in a state of suffering. I learnt to forgive my late husband for not being the person that I wanted him to be and in so doing learnt also to forgive myself. I was as God created me so there was no need for me to feel inadequate in any way. Asking for healing and help was in many ways asking for a change in how I perceived and viewed my path. Wisdom came from experience and greatly freed me from my attachment to getting things done. I learnt to let all pass easily in the knowledge that our higher power was in the driving seat. Once I no longer fought against not knowing I was less confused. I was more centred, full of kindness, open-heartedness, gentleness and the knowledge that intention is what counts.

The best way to serve God is to love all and serve all. So to you who are suffering I say just reach out and receive. I wish you grace for your journey and healing for your heart, and if reading my story has in some way eased your pain then I rejoice with you.

Suggested Reading and Listening

Stephanie Ericsson, *Companion Through the Darkness: Inner Dialogues on Grief,* Hartnolls Ltd, 1993

Louise L. Hay, *You Can Heal Your Life,* Eden Grove Editions, 1984

Louise L. Hay, *The Power is Within You,* Eden Grove Editions, 1991

John McGrath, *Healing and Meditation* [cassette], Available by mail order Tel: +44 (0) 1277 812 482

Martin H. Padovani, *Healing Wounded Emotions,* Twenty-Third Publications, 1991

Colin Murray Parkes, *Bereavement,* London, Pelican Books, 1987